THE

WYNNES

OF SLIGO & LEITRIM

WINSTON GUTHRIE-JONES

Acknowledgements:

The Author and Publishers gratefully acknowledge the assistance of Sligo County Library, Sligo Family Research Society and Leitrim County Library.

The map of County Sligo was prepared by John O'Hara and is reproduced by kind permission of Sligo Family Research Society. The map of County Leitrim is reproduced by kind permission of the County Librarian.

Cover Design: Eyecon

Published in Ireland in 1994   by
Drumlin Publications

© Winston Guthrie-Jones

ISBN   1 873437 07 2

Published by Drumlin Publications, Nure, Manorhamilton, Co. Leitrim, Ireland (072) 55237
Printed by The Sligo Champion

Contents

To my step-children Guy and Fiona L'Estrange, great-grand children of Owen Wynne the Last.

Preface

This book attempts to trace the history of the Sligo family of Wynne of Hazelwood from its origins in 12th century Wales to its extinction, due to the failure of male heirs, in 1910. The then head of the family left Wales and established himself in Ireland in 1658, so that the larger part of the book, which is concerned with Ireland, covers a period of nearly three hundred years. The Hazelwood estate, with which the family is principally associated, was acquired in 1722.

The primary sources on which this history is based consist of four collections of manuscripts. The first is a collection of documents, particularly letters, and papers relating to the property, which is in the possession of the present day members of the family. The documents quoted from this collection are here published for the first time. Secondly, the Public Record Office in Belfast has four volumes of documents relating to the service of the family in the Wars of William III and Marlborough. Thirdly, the manuscripts, printed books and newspapers in the Sligo County Library contain much information about the family. Fourthly, the National Library of Ireland has a collection of Wynne papers, chiefly conveyances and estate accounts.

References to Wood-Martin and O'Rorke refer to their respective histories (published in 1882 and 1889) of the town and County of Sligo.

For three hundred years, the head of the Wynne family, with one exception, bore the forename of Owen. In this book those named Owen have been numbered I to VI. The exception is John Arthur Wynne whose elder brother was named Owen but who died young within the lifetime of his father.

The family of Wynne belonged to the ascendancy. Today, as in previous centuries in Ireland, landlordism has a bad name but like its counterpart, industrial capitalism, it contributed to the economic development of western Europe. However, the landlord-tenant rela-

tionship cannot be equitable or even stable unless it is based on recip-
rocal rights and duties. Regrettably in Ireland, because landlordism
did not evolve internally but was imposed by conquest from outside,
this balance did not always exist, so that the tenant was at the landlord's mercy (or lack of it). But some landlords, among whom were
the Wynnes, were genuinely devoted to the welfare of their tenants,
while the improvements in agriculture effected by the family indirect-
ly benefited the whole rural community.

In order to obtain a rough idea of changes in the value of money
over the centuries one should multiply 18th century figures by 200
and figures for the end of the 19th and beginning of the 20th centuries
by 50.

Culleenamore,
Sligo.
October 1993

HAZELWOOD HOUSE AT THE END OF THE 19TH CENTURY.
PHOTO: COURTESY OF THE NATIONAL LIBRARY OF IRELAND

CHAPTER ONE

Welsh Ancestry

The family of Wynne with which this book is concerned came to Ireland from Wales in 1658 after acquiring extensive lands around Lurganboy, Co. Leitrim. Their home in Wales had been at Bala in the old county of Merioneth, now part of the larger county of Gwynedd.

The family was prominent in that part of Wales. They owned nearly 2000 acres stretching along the northern shore of Lake Bala. Their house was Plas-yn-dre situated at the centre of the little township. The country was sheep-raising, the wool being used for the cottage industry of spinning and weaving, while the bulk of it was carried on pack-horses to the English markets at Oswestry and Shrewsbury.

The family of Plas-yn-dre traced its ancestry back through ten generations to a 12th century chieftain named Rhirid Flaidd ('Rhirid the Wolf'). Rhirid received bardic praise for killing Saxons, as the Welsh called the invaders of their country. True, the rank and file were Saxons but their leaders were the far more formidable Norman lords. Chieftains, like Rhirid and his contemporary Owen Gwynedd, who styled himself Prince, and their descendants succeeded in beating off the Normans during a period of a hundred and fifty years until in 1282 King Edward I conquered the whole of Wales and killed the last independent Prince of Wales in battle.

The descendants of Owen Gwynedd became the family of Wynn of Gwydir. Gwydir Castle, built in about 1500, stands on the river Conwy near the town of Llanrwst. By 1600 the head of the family of Gwydir was Sir John Wynn, one of the Welsh magnates who rose to power while the Tudors wore the crown. The families of Plas-yn-dre and Gwydir twice intermarried. On the second occasion Lewis Gwynne of Plas-yn-dre (the names Gwynne and Wynne are interchangeable) married the niece of Sir John Wynne. Lewis's eldest son was Owen Wynne, the subject of the next chapter, who obtained the grant of land in Ireland and became the ancestor of the Wynnes of Hazelwood.

The coat of arms of the Wynne family displays three wolves' heads on the shield. These refer to the wolf in Rhirid Flaidd's name and they are found in the arms of other families descended from the same ancestor . The Wynne's motto is "Non sibi sed toti" — " not for oneself but for all."

After a hundred and fifty years the Wynnes of Hazelwood forgot the details of their Welsh origins until in about 1800 when the then Owen Wynne and his brothers enquired into the matter. This was done partly out of a natural interest in knowing who were their forbears and partly because it was thought that Owen might just be entitled to the Gwydir baronetcy. There was no foundation for this belief. Nevertheless their researchers led them back to Owen Gwynedd and Rhirid Flaidd, ancestors of whom they must have felt justifiably proud.

GWYDIR, LLANRSWST, WALES

CHAPTER TWO

Owen Wynne I
of Lurganboy, Co. Leitrim
Died 1670

It is important to notice that Owen Wynne I, who was the first of the family to settle in Ireland, was not a younger son who, having no property in England or Wales, set out to make his fortune abroad. He was the eldest child of Lewis Gwynne. In addition to such land as he acquired in Ireland, he was after his father's death the owner of the estate at Bala. He continued to own the Bala property until the time of his own death and it was not until his son James had succeeded him that the property was sold. The question arises why a Welsh landowner should choose to leave Wales for a new life in Ireland. The answer lies in the fact that Owen's influential friends amongst the Cromwellians offered him Irish lands even more extensive than those which he already owned in Wales.

The principle behind the Cromwellian settlement of Irish land was quite different from that of James I's plantations. Where a plantation was effected it was the duty of the new landowner to settle Protestant tenants on the land. Hence comes the Protestant population of Ulster, for the most part lowland Scots in origin. Under Cromwell a Catholic peasantry was to be left as it was; dispossession was of the Catholic landowners. Those Catholic landowners who had taken part in the rising between 1641 and the arrival of Cromwell in 1649 forfeited their lands, those who had taken no part in the rising were to be removed to Connaught and Clare where they could hold land in compensation for their land elsewhere which was expropriated. Thus large areas of land became available for the 'adventurers' who had invested in the Cromwellian conquest and for soldiers who had fought in the Commonwealth army. Although the policy was not fully achieved, it succeeded in creating, not a Protestant community, but a Protestant land-owning class. As to land owned by the church, this was declared to be the property of Parliament. It was let to supporters of the parliamentary cause in the form of large areas of church land which these head lessees sub-let for their own benefit. Although such land reverted to the Church of Ireland at the Restoration, it continued to be subject to the head tenancies which Parliament had granted.

Lewis Gwynne of Bala and his family were supporters of the parliamentary side in the English Civil War. One of the parliamentary leaders was Col. John Jones, Cromwell's brother-in-law. Jones had been born at Maes-y-Garnedd, a farm in the hills between Barmouth and Harlech in the same county as Bala. There is no doubt that Col. Jones and Lewis Gwynne knew each other. In 1648 Sir Owen Wynn of Gwydir wrote to the colonel asking him to do any good office which he was able to do on behalf of Lewis Gwynne of Bala. The colonel replied that he would do so. Sir Owen Wynn, who had succeeded to his father's baronetcy, was a first cousin of Lewis Gwynne's wife.

Col. Jones became prominent in the Cromwellian administration of Ireland. Between 1650 and 1654 he was one of the six parliamentary commissioners who ruled the country, and at the end of the Commonwealth he was the head of the parliamentary army in Ireland. It was at that latter stage that he bestowed a considerable benefit on the Bala family by prompting Richard Cromwell, who succeeded his father as Lord Protector, to grant in 1658 to Owen Wynne I two leases of church land in County Leitrim, one of land belonging to the See of Kilmore and the other of land belonging to the See of Ardagh. Such grants were called bishops' leases. Ten years later in 1668 Owen Wynne II bought for £750 from John Abercromby of Ballinaleck, County Fermanagh, a further 1000 acres in County Leitrim. But the bulk of the Wynne property in the latter county remained the land which was comprised in the bishops' leases. Thus in the 19th century, to anticipate what is said in chapter twelve, the capital value to the Wynnes of the bishops' leases was assessed at £43,000, while the remainder of the Leitrim estate, which consisted of 800 leases at low rents, was estimated to be worth £20,750. The acreage of the bishops' leases was far greater than that of other Wynne property in the county. The total acreage of the Wynne estate in the 19th century in Leitrim

LURGANBOY LODGE, LURGANBOY

was 15,500, of which the only land which we can be sure was bought by the Wynnes was the 1000 acres referred to above. Again, the income derived from the bishops' leases was substantial. John Arthur Wynne in the 19th century made the following calculation of that income:-

Lease held under the See of Kilmore	£2,008
Deduct head rent and several fines (i.e. fixed payments made at agreed intervals).	301
	£1,707
Lease held under the See of Ardagh	£1,459
Deduct as above	261
	£1,198

Thus the net income from the bishops' leases in the 19th century was just short of £3,000 p.a.

The prospect of acquiring the bishops' leases was, then, the reason why the Welsh-speaking Owen left his own country and sailed to

11

Ireland. He established himself there in a remarkably short time. He was High Sheriff, under the Commonwealth, of Leitrim and Roscommon in 1659 and again of Leitrim in 1663. The Wynne house in Lurganboy, named Lurganboy Lodge, which still stands in that small town, was probably built by him. He married Catherine, daughter of Lord Strabane, son of the Earl of Abercorn and Lady Sarah Gordon, daughter of the Marquess of Huntly. Through Lady Sarah there is a relationship with the House of Stuart. O'Rorke says of Lady Sarah Gordon that she got into great trouble by her previous marriage to the ill-fated Sir Phelim O'Neill, who had been an instigator of the rising of 1641 and who was executed by Cromwell. The Earl of Abercorn had been one of the Scottish undertakers of the Ulster plantation. He was a pioneer in agriculture and had built the first village at Belfast.

After the Restoration Owen Wynne held the rank of colonel in the army of Charles II. When he succeeded his Welsh father in 1663 he was the owner of the family estate in Wales together with the bishops' leases of the church lands in County Leitrim. At his death his personal property in Ireland, including livestock, was valued at £532, a figure which excludes the value of the land. He left four sons and three daughters, of whom the eldest son James and the third son Owen, the first Wynne of Hazelwood, are the subject of the two following chapters. His benefactor, Col. John Jones, through whose influence Owen Wynne had obtained the bishops' leases, expected little mercy at Charles II's restoration, for he had been one of the parliamentarians who had signed the death warrant of Charles I, and for that he was tried and executed in September, 1660. He faced his trial and sentence with dignity and fortitude.

CHAPTER THREE

WAR 1688 - 1713

With hardly a break the states of Europe were at war during the closing years of the 17th century and the opening years of the 18th century in an attempt to curb the military aggression of Louis XIV of France. Members of the Wynne family who fought in these wars were Owen Wynne I's three sons, namely James, Lewis and Owen II, and his three grandsons, namely James' son, also called James, and Lewis' two sons, Owen Wynne III and John.

In the history of England and Ireland the year 1688 when William and Mary were offered and accepted the crown is, of course, of crucial importance. Already William, as the stadtholder of the Dutch Republic, had been at war with Louis for some years, for Louis' purpose was to destroy the republic and ruin its trade. The motives which lay behind the 'Glorious Revolution' of 1688 were mixed. The Whig grandees who expelled James II and replaced him on the throne by William and Mary were determined to thwart James' policy of reverting to Stuart absolutism and, if possible, restoring Catholicism as the state religion. In no way would the oligarchy which ruled England permit the restoration of Catholicism, partly because the title to their land depended on the reformation settlement, but also because Catholicism was associated with political absolutism. Nor could they shut their eyes to Louis' revocation of the Edict of Nantes in the very year in which James had ascended the throne, with the subsequent persecution and cruelties to which the Protestants of France had been subjected. To William, on the other hand, his possession of the English crown represented a considerable accession of strength in the war against Louis. In addition William feared that, judging by their recent history, the English were quite capable of deposing James and replacing him with a commonwealth, thus repeating the history of Charles I. William could not forget that during the Commonwealth England had been an ally of Louis in his war with the Dutch, for at that time the English, too, had seen how advantageous to them it

13

would be if Dutch trade could be destroyed.

The 'War of the Two Kings' in Ireland, following James' disembarkation at Kinsale in March, 1689, was but one aspect of the European struggle. James' army consisted in part of French troops, while William's army had many contingents of Protestant French, Dutch, Germans and Danes. From James' point of view, if he won the war in Ireland he could take his army over to Scotland, join up with his supporters there under the Earl of Dundee and thence invade England and try to regain his throne. Louis' purpose was expressed in the following words addressed by his ambassador to James:

> 'Ireland was to be severed from the English crown, purged of English colonists, re-united to the Church of Rome, placed under the protection of the House of Bourbon and made in everything but name a French province'.

Except for making Ireland a French province, these words embody the aims of the Irish who fought in James's army. Above all the Irish war offered the opportunity to recover lost land. A Jacobite victory would reverse the Elizabethan conquests, the plantations and the Cromwellian land settlement. Conversely the English, Scottish and Welsh landowners had every reason to fight to retain what they held. The family of Wynne is but one example of those affected. It had established itself in Ireland barely thirty years before the start of the Williamite war. From May to July 1689, at a time when, apart from Derry and Enniskillen, all Ireland was in Jacobite hands, James held a parliament in Dublin. This parliament enacted that Catholic landowners or their heirs should recover the land they had held in 1641. In addition an Act of Attainder was directed at those in Ireland who had joined the Williamite cause. The list of those attained contained 1,340 names headed by the Duke of Ormond and the Archbishop of Dublin. It contained the names of James Wynne of Lurganboy and his brothers, Lewis and Owen. Those whose names were on the list were declared traitors and liable to the usual punishments of death and confiscation.

Thus the stakes were high. The fate of Irish Catholics in the event of a Williamite victory is expressed by Macaulay in his History in the following words:

14

The priest who had just taken possession of the glebe and the chancel, the Catholic squire who had just been carried back on the shoulders of his shouting tenantry into the hall of his fathers, would be driven forth to live on such alms as peasants, themselves depressed and miserable, could spare. These apprehensions provided such an outbreak of patriotic and religious enthusiasm as deferred for a time the inevitable day'.

After the inevitable day and the defeat of the Jacobite forces in Ireland, William pursued the conflict with Louis in the Netherlands. There the war dragged on for nine years during which James Wynne died of wounds received in battle. After William's death in 1702 war against France was resumed on a wider scale, extending beyond the Netherlands to Spain, Italy, North America and the West Indies. In the next three chapters we shall see something of the service of the Wynne family in the army of William in Ireland and on the continent, and later during the war of the Spanish Succession in the army of the Duke of Marlborough.

CHAPTER FOUR

Brigadier - General James Wynne
Died 1695

BRIGADIER - GENERAL JAMES WYNNE

J ames Wynne of Lurganboy, the eldest son of Owen Wynne I, succeeded his father in 1670. He held the office of High Sheriff for County Leitrim in 1686 and was Member of Parliament for the same county in 1692. He married Catherine, daughter of John Bingham of Castlebar. John Bingham had married James Wynne's mother as her third husband, his daughter Catherine, whom James married, being a child of Bingham's by a previous marriage. The family of Bingham had been prominent in the Elizabethan wars in Ireland and in particular had contested the possession of Sligo castle with the forces of Hugh Roe O'Neill.

Catherine Wynne née Bingham

In 1681 James Wynne sold the Bala estate to his neighbour Simon Lloyd of Rhiwaedog for £1,400. The purchaser's grandson, the Rev. Simon Lloyd (1756-1836) rebuilt the old Play-yn-dre. After being altered in several respects in the 19th century, the house was converted into a hotel in 1990. The hotel bears the name of Plas-yn-dre and displays as its sign the arms of the Wynne family.

When William landed at Torbay in November, 1688, King James fled to France and did not land in Ireland until March of the following day. In these early days, before the arrival of troops from England under the Duke of Schomberg in the autumn of 1689 and under William in June 1690, the war in Ireland had already begun. All Ireland, with the exception of the Protestant enclaves of Derry and Enniskillen, both of which harboured Protestant refugees from the surrounding counties, was in Jacobite hands. The starting point of the conflict may be found in December, 1688, when thirteen apprentice boys closed the gates of Derry against a Jacobite army. The siege of Derry had begun.

James Wynne left Ireland for England to enlist in William's army. We shall see in chapter seven that this is what his brother Lewis did, and perhaps they went together. According to Dalton's English Army Lists, James was appointed a captain in Col. Cunningham's regiment of foot. In April, 1689 this regiment, together with a second regiment under a Col. Richards, sailed from Liverpool in ten troopships destined for the relief of the besieged Derry. The voyage of six days was appalling. The men were unable to lie down and sleep, the biscuit, which had been in store in Chester castle since Monmouth's rebellion four years earlier, was rotten and mouldy and "the beer stank so that

17

the men chose rather to drink salt water or their own urine". Many died. On arrival at Lough Foyle these two regiments were turned back by Lundy, the governor of Derry, on the ground that there were not enough provisions to feed them. Opinions differ as to whether Lundy was a traitor bent on handing over the city to James or whether he was merely massively incompetent. He escaped from Derry in disguise during the siege and his effigy is still burnt annually in the city. In the event the two regiments sailed back to England, where Cunningham and Richards were arrested and dismissed from the service.

At the end of May Major-General Kirke sailed from England with four regiments for the relief of Derry. Two of these regiments were those which had been engaged in the abortive attempt at relief under Cunningham and Richards. Cunningham's own regiment was now commanded by Col. Stewart and James Wynne was serving in it in his previous rank of captain. On arrival at Lough Foyle, Kirke inexcusably delayed relieving the city, believing that without a serious loss of ships he could not break the boom built by the Jacobites across the river. When eventually Kirke broke through the boom the siege had lasted for over three months and those who were left in the city were in the closing stages of starvation.

While the siege lasted the Enniskilleners constantly harried James' line of supply between Dublin and Derry. The Enniskilleners had 17 troops of horse, 30 foot companies and a few troops of dragoons, but they suffered from a lack of adequate arms. They sent two representatives to Kirke to ask for help. The two went by sea from Ballyshannon to the island of Inch in Lough Swilly where they met Kirke. One of the Enniskilleners was Andrew Hamilton who in 1690 published his *True Relation of the Action of the Enniskillen Men*. In this book Hamilton describes how Kirke gave them firearms, powder and some small cannons. He continues:

> "The Major-General told us that he could spare none of his private men, but gave us some very good officers, viz Colonel William Wolseley to be our commander-in-chief and Colonel William Berry to be lieutenant-colonel of our horse, Captain Charles Stone to be major of our horse and Captain James Wynne, a gentleman from Ireland, but then a captain in

Colonel Stewart's regiment, to be colonel of our dragoons. And
for our three regiments of foot, Gustavus Hamilton, governor
of Enniskillen, was made eldest colonel, and Lt-Colonel Lloyd
and Major Tiffan were the other two colonels".

This little group of officers, namely Wolseley, Berry, Stone and
Wynne, together with the two emissaries from Enniskillen, sailed
from Inch to Ballyshannon while the arms followed in other vessels.
From Ballyshannon the group travelled to Belleek and then by boat
up Lower Lough Erne to Enniskillen. There the whole garrison turned
out and men, women and children crowded round them. On the same
day Kirke's warship, the Mountjoy, broke the boom and raised the
siege of Derry.

James Wynne, now promoted colonel, did not have long to wait
for action. A Jacobite army under Justin McCarty, Lord Mountcashel,
an able and honourable man, was advancing on Enniskillen from the
east. Its forward troops were battering at Crom Castle, an outpost of
Enniskilleners at the east end of Upper Lough Erne. Wolseley at once
sent Berry with a few hundred dragoons, horse and foot to the relief
of Crom. This Berry succeeded in doing in a brisk skirmish. Wolseley
followed from Enniskillen with the main body of troops. He learnt
that Mountcashel with an army numbering 4,000 had reached Newtownbutler, a few miles from Crom Castle. Although Wolseley had
about half that number of men, he decided to advance to battle. To the
west and east of Newtownbutler lay a bog bisected by causeways
running into the town. Wolseley's army advanced on the town from
the west. Berry, at the head of the horse, advanced along the causeway, while Tiffan with the foot slogged through the bog on the right,
and Lloyd did the same on the left. Wynne's dragoons, divided into
two parts, advanced with Tiffan and Lloyd on foot. Mountcashel
retreated through the town and set it on fire. About a mile on the
other side of the town he took up a well-chosen site on a hill. Wolseley's forces adopted the same formation as before. This time,
however, his cavalry could not advance along the causeway because
of fire from Mountcashel's cannon. Wolseley's foot, with Wynne's
dismounted dragoons, plodded through the bog and engaged the
enemy. The Irish infantry fought bravely until they saw their cavalry

retreating. This retreat may have been due to a misunderstanding of orders as between 'right face', meaning ride to the assistance of the right wing, and 'right about face', meaning retreat. The result was that the Jacobite foot began to run, the cannons were captured, and the Enniskillen horse thundered over the causeway. Macaulay describes the ensuing scene:

> *The conquerors now gave loose to that ferocity which has seldom failed to disgrace the civil wars of Ireland. The butchery was terrible. Near 1,500 of the vanquished were put to the sword. About 500 more, in ignorance of the country, took a road which led to Lough Erne. The lake was before them: the enemy behind: they plunged into the waters and perished there'.*

It is important to bear in mind that the Battle of Newtownbutler was fought before the arrival of Williamite troops from England. Schomberg, William's commander-in-Chief, landed in Ireland about two months after the battle, while William himself did not come until the middle of the following year. When Newtownbutler was fought the Battle of the Boyne lay nearly twelve months ahead.

When Schomberg took command in Ireland he sent a number of written orders to Wynne relating to the deployment of Wynne's dragoons. These orders are with the Wynne papers in the P.R.O. in Belfast. In particular one troop of horse was to be stationed at Ballyshannon to patrol the road to Sligo, then held by the Jacobites. On Schomberg's arrival the bulk of the Enniskilleners joined him at Dundalk. One of Schomberg's entourage noted in his diary:

> *"The arrival of the so-called Enniskilling dragoons increased the number of the army but not its mutual harmony. The sight of their thin little nags and the wretched dress of their riders, half-naked with sabres and pistols hanging from their belts, looked like a horde of Tartars. These brave people offered themselves as volunteers for the advance guard. They could not bear to be given orders, but kept saying that they were no good if they were not allowed to act as they pleased. This was such a contrast to*

Schomberg's strict discipline that he decided to make an
exception and let them go according to their own genius".

Wynne's dragoons, however, appear to have joined Schomberg's
army only shortly before the Battle of the Boyne and after they had
been deployed widely as patrols. Gideon Bonnivert, a Frenchman
serving in Schomberg's army, described their arrival:

"We encamped in very rugged ground (near Dundalk). The
Enniskillen Dragoons came there to us. They are but middle
sized men, but they are nevertheless brave fellows. I have
seen them like mastiff dogs run against bullets".

The Enniskilleners fought at the Battle of the Boyne on the 1st
July, 1690 (Old Style). Only a brief account of the battle, in so far as
it concerned the Enniskilleners, need be given. The first Williamite
troops to wade across the river were the Dutch Blue Guards, who
attacked the Jacobites entrenched in the village of Oldbridge. Thereafter William committed his troops across the river in successive
stages. First the Enniskilleners, horse and foot, crossed in the wake of
the Dutch Blue Guards. There followed at other crossing places, each
further downstream, the Huguenot regiments and the English foot, the
Dutch foot, the Danish regiments and finally William with the cavalry
and Wynne's dragoons. Once south of the river the Enniskillen foot,
under Col. Gustavus Hamilton, fired volleys of musketry into the
Jacobite cavalry sweeping to the attack of the Huguenot foot. Of the
original squadron of 60 troopers of Jacobite horse, only six to eight
survived this fire. When the Duke of Schomberg crossed the river,
about two hours after the original crossing, he took over the direction
of the Enniskillen and Huguenot regiments. While doing so this old
soldier, aged 75, was killed in a Jacobite charge. In the same charge
George Walker, a hero of the siege of Derry and by now Bishop of
Derry, was also killed. When the Jacobites retreated to the hill of
Donore, south of Oldbridge, William put himself at the head of
Wolseley's Enniskillen horse in the assault on the hill, saying: "Gentleman, you shall be my guards today. I have heard much of you. Let
me see something of you". The Jacobite cavalry, after having with-
drawn southwards from the hill, counter-attacked the pursuing
Enniskillen cavalry, routed them with considerable losses and drove

them back onto the Danish cavalry. In the confusion Enniskilleners and Danes mistook each other for enemies and further losses were suffered. Wynne's dragoons charged the enemy horse with such vigour that they themselves were soon in trouble, having galloped too far in pursuit, but they rallied and returned to engage the enemy infantry. Eventually, the whole Jacobite army was in retreat.

It is worth noting that in the wars in Ireland up to this point many of James Wynne's relations had been engaged in the fighting, not always on the same side. James' mother was the grand-daughter of James Hamilton, first Earl of Abercorn. The latter's descendants, cousins of James Wynne, included Gustavus Hamilton, governor of Enniskillen and the Enniskilleners' commander at the Boyne, and Lt-General Richard Hamilton commander of the besieging forces at Derry and commander of the Jacobite foot at the Boyne. Richard's brothers, Anthony and John were both Major-Generals in the Jacobite forces at Derry. James Wynne's own nephew, Lord Strabane, had arrived outside the walls of Derry during the siege demanding surrender. His language is said to have been so violent that some of the more timid Protestants at once left to make their submission to King James.

The Belfast papers give some indication of the deployment of Wynne's dragoons after the Boyne. In April and May of the following year detachments were at Ballyshannon and Belturbet at a time when Sligo was still in Jacobite hands. In June Wynne's dragoons were among the forty squadrons of cavalry and dragoons which, in addition to thirty battalions of infantry, were assembled by the Williamite commander, Ginkel, for the purpose of forcing the crossing of the Shannon at Athlone. Athlone fell on the 30th June, 1691. On the 12th July St. Ruth, the Jacobite commander, offered battle at Aughrim, twenty miles south-west of Athlone. St. Ruth drew up his army on a ridge running south-east from the castle and village of Aughrim. Between the two armies the land was mostly bog, but on either wing harder ground supported a causeway or rough track. That at the northern end is the old Ballinasloe to Loughrea road, now superseded by a modern by-pass. In a battle which claimed 4,000 men killed on the Jacobite side and about half that number on the Williamite side, the breakthrough took place by the advance of the Williamite cavalry and dragoons along the northern causeway following an artillery bombardment. Fourteen squadrons, or about 1000 men, were involved in this advance, with Wynne's dragoons forming one of the squadrons. When St. Ruth rode over in the direction of this break-through to head personally a counter-charge of the French cavalry, he was decapitated by a cannon ball. This event demoralised his army. His cavalry, who had fought with great bravery at the Boyne, rode away. It has been suggested that the wealthier Jacobites who composed the cavalry as opposed to the infantry had by now more to gain from compromise, and being mounted they had the means to withdraw. In terms appropriate to that age, the upper class deserted the lower. Once the break-through was effected the Jacobite flank could be rolled up from its left. Aughrim was the last battle of the war and the last major battle to be fought in Ireland.

The Green Fort at Sligo, which stood on the hill behind the site of the present-day hospital, still held out for the Jacobites under a redoubtable 70 year old hunchback named Teige O'Regan, who had been knighted by James and who with great resource and courage had held Sligo for fifteen months. In July, 1691, Colonel Mitchelburne advanced towards Sligo from Ballyshannon while Lord Granard with troops who had fought at Aughrim reached Boyle and crossed the Curlew mountains. In these closing stages Col. Wynne's dragoons were engaged in action for the last time in Ireland. Mitchelburne dispatched Col. Ramsay with 100 foot, 400 militia and 200 horse and dragoons from Enniskillen via Dromahaire to Ballysadare. This force moved on to the Barony of Tireragh, the land lying between the Ox mountains and the sea, where they seized a quantity of horses, cattle and sheep. Sir Teige, with the much smaller force of 200 foot and 80 horse, marched from Sligo to the bridge at Ballysadare to intercept Ramsay on his return. A fierce encounter took place. Sir Teige was getting the upper hand when Ramsay was re-inforced by 200 of Wynne's dragoons. The defenders of Sligo retreated helter-skelter and were chased to the Green Fort by Wynne's dragoons. Thirty Jacobites were killed. Sir Teige only avoided capture because he was mistaken for the servant of a Jacobite storekeeper. He remarked: "If they ever catched Sir Teige so far again he would agree to be cracked as a hog cracks a potato".

The end came when Mitchelburne captured the outworks of the Green Fort and Lord Granard advanced from Ballysadare. Sir Teige surrendered. The garrison was allowed to march out with full honours of war, with their arms and baggage, drums beating, colours flying, match lighted and bullets in their mouths. Old Teige made his way to Limerick where he took advantage of the treaty signed on the 3rd October and sailed to France hoping to fight another day on the side of Louis.

The Belfast papers show us something of James Wynne's subsequent career in the service of William. In April 1694, together with his regiment, he left Ireland for Flanders. In October of that year, while serving at Ghent, he was promoted Brigadier-General. In June of the following year John Pain, the regimental agent in England, wrote to Wynne expressing regret at the news that the latter had been wounded in action. Three months later Pain wrote to James' younger brother, Lt-Col. Owen Wynne, also serving in Flanders, expressing condolences on James' death. He had died of wounds at Roeselare, now a sizeable Belgian town. Both Wood-Martin and O'Rorke in their respective histories of Sligo (the latter copying from the former) are in error in saying that James was killed at the Battle of Malplaquet, an event which did not take place until 1709.

Thus died a gallant soldier. He was about 50 years of age. He had been chosen by Kirke at Inch as one of his best officers and had been promoted from captain to colonel to command a regiment of dragoons. The calibre of the officers sent from Inch to Enniskillen is demonstrated by the quality of Wolseley and Berry who accompanied Wynne. Col. Wolseley generously ascribed his success at the Battle of Newtownbutler to the excellence of his officers and the marksmanship of his men.

Before leaving James Wynne it is appropriate to add a further word about Wynne's dragoons and their subsequent history. Dragoons were by origin a body of mounted infantry who could be moved rapidly on a field of battle. Their principal weapon was the carbine, a shorter weapon than the infantry musket. They were less well mounted

24

than cavalry and fought normally on foot, often firing on a cavalry charge from behind a hedge or similar cover. At Naseby, the decisive battle of the English civil war, having done just that, the dragoons mounted and charged an exposed flank of the King's infantry. After the Williamite wars, when Wynne's dragoons fought in Marlborough's army on the continent, the regiment was known as the 5th Royal Irish Dragoons. It was heavily engaged in the principal battles of Blenheim, Ramillies, Oudenarde and Malplaquet, and these battles are among its battle honours. In 1713, at the end of the war, the regiment was placed on the establishment of Ireland, but from then until 1799 there was a steady decline in its efficiency. It was split up in small detachments and billeted in public houses and similar accommodation where the supervision of the officers was ineffective. By the time of the rising of 1798 it had been infiltrated by subversive elements disloyal to the Crown. Although these soldiers were discovered and executed, George III ordered the whole regiment's disbandment in 1799.

Fifty-nine years later in 1858 the order to disband was cancelled and the regiment was re-constituted as the 5th Royal Irish Lancers. It thereafter served with distinction, and a number of battles of the first world war are among its battle honours. In 1922 the regiment was amalgamated with the 16th Lancers; because of its break in service it was junior to the 16th Lancers, so that the new title became the 16th/5th Lancers. In 1940, while in India during the second world war, the amalgamated regiment was mechanised, after which it served in North Africa in the 6th Armoured Division. In 1959 Queen Elizabeth approved the title of The 16th/5th The Queen's Royal Lancers. In the Gulf War of 1991 the regiment formed part of the 7th Armoured Brigade, one of the two armoured brigades in the British 1st Armoured Division. The British government announced in 1992 that the strength of the British army was to be reduced and that a number of regiments were to be amalgamated. The 16th/5th The Queen's Royal Lancers is to be amalgamated with the 17th/21st Lancers, and the title of the Queen's Royal Lancers is to apply to the newly formed regiment.

25

CHAPTER FIVE

Lieutenant - General Owen Wynne II
1664-1737

LIEUTENANT - GENERAL OWEN WYNNE

Owen Wynne II, the third son of Owen Wynne I of Lurganboy, was born in 1664 or 1665. He was educated at Trinity college, Dublin, and studied for the Bar. In 1689 he was a captain in the Earl of Roscommon's Regiment of Foot and in the following year fought with the Williamite forces at the Boyne. He left Ireland for Flanders with his brother James' regiment in April, 1694. In November of that year the regimental agent in London, John Pain, wrote to Brig-General James Wynne to say that Owen was held at Calais as a prisoner-of-war of the French. Later in the same month Pain wrote again to James Wynne, then at Ghent, to say that an exchange of prisoners was to take place, adding 'we have twenty of theirs to one of ours held by them'. Pain wrote again in December to say that Owen, now promoted major, had landed with other officers at Margate, that he had travelled to London and that he had had a meeting with Pain. Thereafter Owen returned to the continent and served with Colonel Charles Ross's Regiment of dragoons, a regiment which had been Wynne's dragoons until James Wynne was promoted to Brigadier-General. He continued to serve in Flanders until the Peace of Ryswick in 1697 brought a temporary lull in hostilities.

We get so few glimpses of the private lives of the Wynnes that it is worth mentioning that the Belfast records contain two letters to Owen written in French from a Guillaume Beert at Cambrai (the town that gave its name to cambric) relating to the price of lace which Beert had to sell. Either Owen wished to decorate his own clothes in the prevailing 18th century style or, like all soldiers serving abroad, he wanted to send some presents home.

The War of the Spanish Succession began in 1702, the year when Queen Anne ascended the throne. England, Holland and Austria formed an alliance against Louis in order to prevent Louis' grandson and heir from ascending the throne of Spain. If this event took place then on Louis' death France and Spain would be united under one monarch. The allies' candidate for the Spanish throne was an Austrian prince. If the allies were victorious a serious disturbance of the European balance of power would be avoided. The Duke of Marlborough's campaigns were fought mainly in Flanders, but the first of the great set battles, that of Blenheim, was fought far to the south near a village of that name on the upper Danube. This battle deserves our attention, for Owen Wynne, then Lt-Colonel, took part in it in command of his regiment, the 5th Royal Irish Dragoons. As we saw in the last chapter, this was the new name of Wynne's dragoons. Blenheim was fought in August, 1704. In the previous year Bavaria, at first an adherent of the allies, changed sides and joined Louis. At this turn of events Louis, with the help of the Elector of Bavaria, aimed to march down the Danube, capture Vienna, and at one blow knock Austria out of the war. Louis' chances of success were increased by the fact that Austria's Protestant subjects in Hungary were in revolt. Marlborough determined to frustrate this plan. He obtained from the Dutch, nominally in command of the armies in Flanders, permission to take an army south as far as the river Moselle. It was expected that he would then turn right and drive into France but instead, having reached Coblenz where the Moselle flows into the Rhine, he marched straight on past Mainz, Heidelberg and Stuttgart to Ulm on the upper Danube. From there he turned east along the Danube to Donauworth, where he was joined by an Austrian army under the command of Prince Eugene. Marlborough's march had covered 250 miles in five weeks. 'The annals of the British army', wrote Churchill, 'contain no more glorious episode than Marlborough's march from the North Sea to the Danube'. One must picture for oneself this army on the move: foot, cavalry, artillery and the baggage train. The baggage train was made up of four-wheeled carts, drawn by horses or oxen, the wheels being eight feet in diameter, carrying arms, ammunition, tents, field kitchens and all the other paraphernalia of war.

On the 2nd July Marlborough and Eugene stormed the Schellenberg, a strongly fortified hill overlooking Donauworth. Casualties were heavy, but the fortress was captured and entrance to Bavaria gained. Meanwhile two French armies and the Bavarian army were converging on Marlborough and Eugene. The allied armies moved west along the Danube to meet them. In the engagement at Blenheim, 36,000 men from Denmark, Prussia, Holland, Austria, Hanover and Hesse, together with a further 9,000 Englishmen (a portmanteau word to include the inhabitants of England, Ireland and Wales, for the word British cannot be used until the union with Scotland in 1707) won a decisive victory over the French. Many may only know of this battle through Southey's poem 'After Blenheim'. One verse must suffice:

> *They say it was a shocking sight*
> *After the field was won:*
> *For many thousand bodies here*
> *Lay rotting in the sun;*
> *But things like that, you know, must be*
> *After a famous victory'.*

The Blenheim Roll, which is printed in Dalton's English Army Lists, and consists of a list of regiments which took part in the battle, contains the name of the 5th Royal Irish Dragoons with Lt-Col. Owen Wynne as their commander. Wynne received a bounty of £78-10-0 for the battle. This sum may be compared with £600 awarded to the Duke and £27 to those holding the rank of captain. The strategic results of the battle were immense. Vienna was saved; all Bavaria fell to the allies; and the prestige of the French among the armies of Europe was seriously damaged.

In March, 1705, Owen Wynne was appointed Colonel of the 23rd Regiment of Foot, a regiment which was raised in England and which sailed for Flanders in 1708. He was appointed Brig-General in 1706; this promotion probably involved his relinquishing the command of the foot regiment. The 23rd regiment took part in the siege of Lille, a fortress well within the frontiers of France. In this operation James Wynne the younger took a part, a fact which will be referred to in the next chapter. After the fall of Lille, Brig-General Wynne was sent by Marlborough to command the garrison of the fortress.

At the Battle of Malplaquet, fought in 1709, the cavalry of fourteen squadrons contained two squadrons of the 5th Royal Irish Dragoons. That battle opened the way to the siege of Douai, a fortress nearer even than Lille to Paris. Both Marlborough and Eugene took part in the siege while among the British troops was the 23rd Regiment of Foot which Owen had previously commanded. When the war ended in 1713 Owen Wynne held the rank of Major-General. In 1715 he was placed on the staff in Ireland as Colonel of the 9th Royal Irish Dragoons. In 1727 he was promoted to Lieutenant-General and appointed Commander-in-Chief in Ireland. The army in Ireland, of which he became the head, was not an Irish army, for the enlistment of Irish troops, whether Protestant of Catholic, was forbidden. This rule was relaxed towards the middle of the century as the demand for troops to serve abroad increased, but even then Presbyterians were barred until 1780. An Irish Catholic, if of appropriate social standing, could obtain a commission in the cavalry, but not in the infantry until 1793. This army, which was always under strength and over-officered, was a by-word for inefficiency, incompetence and even fraud. Officers, who were appointed through patronage without regard to military efficiency, neglected both discipline and training. Fraud was practised through fictitious muster rolls claiming pay for non-existent soldiers, while the costs claimed for building barracks were inflated.

We cannot tell whether General Wynne was able to introduce a measure of reform into this organisation. As the century wore on the army was depleted by the calls on it to serve abroad in the British forces during the War of American Independence. Its place was taken by voluntary militia and yeomanry regiments which provided the troops available to meet the rising of 1798.

Quite apart from his army service, Owen Wynne II established for himself a foremost position in the north-west of Ireland. He was a member of Parliament for Carrick-on-Shannon in 1692 at a time when a serving soldier, in Ireland or in England, was not excluded from membership. He married a daughter of Robert Miller of Milford, County Mayo, but had no children. In some manner he succeeded in becoming a rich man. He was able in 1720 to buy land in County Cavan for £15,000 from the Duke of Wharton. Wharton's father had been Lord Lieutenant of Ireland and had written the mock Irish words of Lilli-Burlero which, when set to music, became widely popular with the English, both military and civilian, and which, Wharton senior boasted, had sung a King (James II) out of three Kingdoms. The dukedom conferred on the son, who at the end of his life was reduced to beggary, drunkenness and destitution in France, is described in the Dictionary of National Biography as being the most extraordinary creation of an English dukedom on record.

Two years later in 1722 Owen Wynne bought the family's estates in County Sligo for £20,000. The previous history of this land will be considered in chapter seven. The conveyance included parts of the town of Sligo, together with the town's fairs, markets, tolls and customs. These, although profitable, were to cause much trouble and controversy in later years. At Hazelwood he built his house, to the designs of the German architect Richard Cassels, some of whose other buildings are Leinster House, Powerscourt, the dining hall at Trinity and St. John's Church, Sligo.

In the same year, 1722, Owen, then a Major-General, together with his brother John and his brother-in-law, Col. John Ffolliott, were elected burgesses of Sligo. There followed what O'Rorke calls a coup d'etat on a small scale. A previous Provost (an office corresponding to mayor), John de Butts, and the town clerk and recorder, George

Bennett, were expelled from the council by the new Provost and Wynne supporter, Mitchelbourne Knox. O'Rorke writes:

> "The council being thus purged of these obnoxious elements, the Wynnes might now manage it as they liked, the result being that the owner of Hazelwood, for the time being, had the Corporation of Sligo, as completely as his own household, under control; and when vacancies occurred in the body the persons elected were always members, connections, friends or creatures of the Wynne family. While the Wynnes surrounded themselves in this way with their Sligo friends, they took care also to arm their relations living at a distance, - the Coles, Farnhams, Sanders - with the franchises of the borough, in order that if any hostile local combination threatened, it might be crushed with the aid of this friendly family reserve'.

The result was that parliamentary elections in the borough of Sligo became merely a matter of form, the choice of member being fixed beforehand at Hazelwood. Although the county was not quite so obviously in the pocket of the Wynne family, yet the family influence was great enough to secure one of its members for one of the two county seats. Owen II himself sat for the borough from 1713 to 1727 when, before the purchase of Hazelwood, his address was given as Lurganboy, and for the county from 1727 to his death in 1737. In succeeding chapters reference will be made to particular elections, but one may here generalise by saying that one of the borough seats was always held by a Wynne from 1715 to 1806 and one of the county seats from 1727 to 1790.

Owen Wynne II died in 1737. He left his estate to his nephew, Owen Wynne III.

Writing at the beginning of the following century, the Rev. Richard Wynne, brother of Owen Wynne V, stated that General Wynne was offered a peerage but refused it; he (the General) said he would rather be the first of the commoners than the last of the peers. Even if he had accepted a peerage, the title would have become extinct on his death.

CHAPTER SIX

Lewis John and James Wynne

The last two chapters have been concerned with James and Owen Wynne, the two most prominent sons of Owen Wynne I of Lurgan-boy. There were two other sons, namely Lewis and John; and, as previously mentioned, Brigadier-General James Wynne, the subject of chapter four, had a son, who was also named James. Where necessary for the sake of clarity, the latter is referred to as James the younger.

Lewis, like his eldest brother, married a daughter of John Bingham. Like his brothers James and Owen he was attainted by James II's Dublin Parliament. The nature of his support for King William may be judged from a petition or memorial addressed to the Lords Justices of Ireland by his son Owen (who became Owen III of Hazelwood) when the latter was seeking a command in the army. The petition is undated, but it is written after the accession of George I in 1714. It reads as follows:

"That his father (viz Lewis Wynne) appeared very early in the service of his late Majesty King William of Glorious Memory, having left his family and concerns in this Kingdom and joined His Majesty at Salisbury, who was pleased to honour him with a commission as captain, and died in the service at Dundalk Camp. That the greatest part of his father's fortune being in stock, the Irish immediately on his going to serve His Majesty seized all his effects to a very considerable value. That as soon as your memorialist was capable of serving the Crown he went into the service in 1706 and bought a company in April 1708 and served several years in Flanders. That being informed there are several regiments to be raised for His Majesty's service in this Kingdom he is desirous at this juncture to serve His Majesty in the army and therefore humbly entreats your Excellencies' favour for such a command therein as may enable him to show his zeal for His Majesty's service'.

32

The Lords Justices to whom the petition was addressed were persons appointed by the Crown to head the government of Ireland in the absence of the Lord Lieutenant or in circumstances where the King was reluctant to appoint any one man with the full powers of Viceroy. The stock in which Lewis' fortune lay was, of course, livestock. The camp at Dundalk was a graveyard for many Williamite soldiers. It was the main Williamite camp set up by William's commander, the Duke of Schomberg, after the latter had landed with troops from England at Belfast Lough in August, 1689. Schomberg proved excessively cautious and no general advance against the Jacobites was made until William's arrival in June of the following year. Meanwhile during the winter of 1689/90 at Dundalk the weather was bad, and the Jacobites had devastated the surrounding land. The troops suffered from fever and dysentery, made worse by a shortage of physicians and medicines. Some 2,000 died in that camp; even more died after being evacuated to a hospital at Belfast; and nearly 1,000 died while being transported back to England. Lewis Wynne was among these casualties.

John Wynne, Lewis' second son, served in the Netherlands in the regiment of his uncle, Owen Wynne II. Burke says of him that he was a man of marked ability but was remarkably extravagant, but no evidence to support this proposition appears amongst the records. He also served in his uncle's regiment in the continental wars under Marlborough. A document in the Belfast records shows that in 1715, at the time of the first Jacobite rising in England John went to England hoping to enlist in the army of George I, but all the available commissions had been filled. Later he petitioned for a captaincy and eventually became Lt-Colonel of the Royal Irish Dragoons, very much a family regiment. He was M.P. for Castlebar from 1727 to 1747.

In the Netherlands John's cousin, James the younger, served as a captain in his uncle Owen's 23rd Regiment of Foot. We have one glimpse of him in 1708 from a letter in the Belfast records written by a fellow officer, Captain Henry Crawford. When the allies were besieging Lille they maintained a line of supply to that fortress from Ostend, where supplies brought from England were landed. The town of Lessigne lay on this route; it had a castle which it was important for the allies to hold against flank attacks by the French. The French had flooded the land to the south-west of Ostend so that much of the supplies for the besiegers of Lille had to be ferried by boat. On the 14th October, 1708, James Wynne the younger, in command of one hundred Grenadiers, arrived with Captain Crawford at Lessigne. The castle, which lay at a short distance from the town, was under the command of a Col. Caulfied. Caulfield was under attack by the French, and was determined to surrender. As Wynne and his troops approached the castle they were met by musket fire from the French who had occupied a nearby graveyard. Caulfield ordered James not to return the fire. The colonel, with such troops as he had, then marched out of the castle and surrendered as prisoners of war. It is not clear from Capt. Crawford's letter whether he, James and the Grenadiers succeeded in avoiding capture or not.

James the younger was the heir to the family lands in County Leitrim, for he was the son of Owen I's eldest son. One would have thought that his inheritance on his father's death in 1695 was substantial, for his father had not only inherited Owen I's property but had also sold the Welsh estate. And yet James the younger was penniless, for his father died insolvent. On the 8th November, 1707, twelve years after his father's death, James signed a document which read as follows:

> *'Know all men by these presents that I, James Wynne of Lurganboy, son and heir of James Wynne of Lurganboy, deceased, having maturely considered the many and great debts contracted by my father in his life time and which were left unpaid at the time of his death as also the insufficiency of the estate and assets by him left for paying the said debts and for maintaining of me and my sisters Dorothy, Sidney, Jane and Mary Wynne. I gratefully acknowledge the kindness of my uncle Owen Wynne of Ballinow* (Ballina?) *in the County of Mayo, Esquire, in taking upon him the administration of my said father's goods and chattels and the guardianship of me during my minority and being fully satisfied that the sum of money by him expended paying my said fathers' debts, in maintaining of me and my sisters and portioning of my sister Dorothy, do far exceed the sum of money he had or might have received as executor or guardian as*

34

aforesaid. Do therefore hereby exonerate, discharge, release and forever quit claim unto the said Owen Wynne, his heirs executors and administrators, of and from all manner of accounts and demands whatsoever from the beginning of the world unto the date of these presents'.

The occasion when this document was signed by James was attended by much solemnity. Five witnesses added their signatures to it. These were John Dunbar, brother-in-law of James senior; Owen Wynne III; John Wynne, who was probably James senior's brother; and John Miller and Francis Cocksedge, relations of the Wynne family by marriage.

The document is drafted in very wide terms. Its effect was to declare that nothing was due to James from his father's estate because of his father's insolvency. The money raised by the sale of the Welsh estate had been spent, while the lands in County Leitrim must have been heavily encumbered. Owen II, who no doubt was making the decisions, could, after paying the debts, have left his nephew James as owner of the land and could have made him his own heir. But Owen II decided that his heir should be, not James, but Owen III, the son of his younger brother Lewis Wynne. In that same year, 1707, James the younger settled on Owen Wynne III the Lurganboy estate including the bishop's leases, while on his death in 1737 Owen II left his property, in particular the newly acquired Hazelwood estate, to Owen III. James and his four sisters simply fade out of the family history.

Owen II may well have thought that all the family property should be concentrated in the hands of one owner rather than that the Leitrim lands should go to one member of the family and the Sligo lands to another. But we do not know why James, who had the strongest claim through being the representative of the senior line, should be passed over. Note the date of Capt. Crawford's letter quoted above. It is one year after the date of James' declaration and the settlement of his estates on Owen III. The fact that in 1708 James the younger was a captain on active service does not suggest that he was unfit to inherit the estates nor that he was incapable of begetting a male heir who would carry on the senior line.

35

CHAPTER SEVEN

The Wynne Estate in County Sligo

Owen Wynne II in 1722 became the owner of about 14,500 acres of land in County Sligo by a conveyance from an English baronet named Sir Francis Leicester. One may discover the previous history of this land from a statement of title prepared for Owen V by his solicitor.

Thomas Wentworth, later Earl of Strafford, was Charles I's Lord Deputy in Ireland from 1633 to 1639. His policy was to advance the interests of the King at the expense of Norman Irish, Catholics and Protestants alike. While engaged in this task neither he nor his secretary, Sir George Radcliffe, were slow to advance their own interests as well. In 1636 Wentworth and Radcliffe, acting through a nominee, bought the lands of Teige O'Connor Sligo which covered the greater part of the county. The subsequent history of the vendor and the purchasers is that the O'Connors Sligo faded into oblivion; Wentworth, recalled to England by the Long Parliament, was attainted and executed in 1641; and Radcliffe died in penury in France during the Commonwealth in the service of the two future Kings, Charles II and James II.

O'Rorke was doubtful whether the sale of the O'Connor Sligo lands in 1636 was a genuine one and thought that the unfortunate O'Connors Sligo were swindled out of their immense estates. Recently more light has been thrown on the matter by Dr. Mary O'Dowd in her book *'Power, Politics and Land: Sligo 1568-1688'*. According to Dr. O'Dowd the O'Connors were victims of misfortune. They had adopted the English law of primogeniture which would have secured the integrity of their estates had it not been for the fact that in the first half of the 17th century the family suffered from a lack of direct male heirs. Thus their estates devolved sideways from brother to brother or even, as in Teige's case, to the uncle of the deceased owner. Each time the estate devolved to a new heir a fine was payable to the Crown, a fine being a sum due when a particular state of affairs came to an end. In addition, in 1636 three widows of previous owners were living, each entitled to a substantial annual sum secured on the estate. Finally Teige's predecessor had mortgaged a large part of the estate to a Galway merchant named French. In these circumstances Teige was anxious to sell the greater part of the estate to Wentworth and Radcliffe, so as to relieve himself of debt, on condition that the purchasers undertook to pay the debts with which the estate was encumbered.

French objected to the sale on the grounds that it deprived him of his security under his mortgage. In 1640 he sailed to England where he presented a petition to the Commons alleging that he had been dispossessed by Wentworth and Radcliffe. Teige followed him to England intending to claim that Wentworth and Radcliffe had not carried out their part of the bargain, but he was shipwrecked and drowned on the voyage. The outbreak of the English civil war swept all such objections into oblivion but it remains true that if the buyers had not kept their part of the bargain, so that Teige was still encumbered with his debts, then Teige was swindled. Unfortunately this was never brought to trial because of Teige's death.

Under the Commonwealth much of the land in Sligo, and elsewhere in Ireland, passed into the hands of new Protestant owners largely by grant rather than by purchase. The Restoration, when Charles II recovered his throne, posed a serious dilemma. Many Irish Catholic landowners had fought for Charles I, and they had every reason to expect from the King's son the restitution of their lands and the tolerance of their religion. Unfortunately Charles II had been recalled from exile by the Army, the creation of Cromwell, and that Army under General Monk insisted that the Cromwellian land settlement in Ireland should be left undisturbed. It was plainly impossible to satisfy all claimants.

The Act of Settlement of 1662 provided that 'Innocents', namely those who had not taken up arms against the English in the rebellion of 1641 to 1649, should be restored to their former estates, and that Cromwellian settlers should be compensated by the grant of land elsewhere of a value equal to that which they had to surrender. This policy proved incapable of being carried into effect. The Act was therefore followed by the Act of Explanation of 1665 which provided that Cromwellians should surrender one-third of their lands and that that third should be available for restoration to the Innocents. Clearly many claimants were left unsatisfied, the Gaelic Irish faring the worst.

Wentworth and Radcliffe were plainly innocent in the statutory sense, so that their heirs, Thomas, 2nd Earl of Strafford, and Thomas Radcliffe, junior, had a very strong claim to the lands once owned by the O'Connors Sligo. The Act of Settlement contained a clause specifically referring to these lands. That clause recited the sale by Teige to Wentworth and Radcliffe, but provided that for the time being the lands were to be vested in the King until the Lord Lieutenant, after hearing the claimants concerned, should adjudge to whom they belonged. The Lord Lieutenant's adjudication was to have the force of law. Accordingly, in 1663 the matter was enquired into by the Lord Lieutenant and the Council of Ireland. Amongst those who nominally disputed the claim of the Wentworth and Radcliffe heirs were the Cromwellian Lord Collooney (Richard Coote) and Martin O'Connor, the grandson of Teige. O'Rorke says that although Martin O'Connor was entered as a petitioner, it would appear that his name was used without his consent for, although Teige's heirs and assigns had been ordered by the Council to make answer, Martin himself does not appear to have done so. It is a pity the Martin did not make answer, for if he had done so he could have challenged the sale on the ground that Wentworth and Radcliff had not kept their promises under their agreement with his grandfather, if such was the case.

In any event he would have had little chance of success because his family had taken a prominent part in the 1641 rebellion. Judgement was given in favour of Wentworth and Radcliffe. The matter was referred to again in six clauses of the Act of Explanation of 1665 which, after reciting the sale by Teige O'Connor Sligo to Wentworth and Radcliffe in 1636, enacted that the adventurers and commissioned officers of the Commonwealth period who were to be removed from the O'Connor Sligo lands should have so much of other forfeited lands as might be sufficient to reprise them for two-thirds of these lands which they had to forfeit. Finally, by letters patent of 1678 the

38

King confirmed the title to the land in the names of the 2nd Earl of Strafford and Thomas Radcliffe junior.

Radcliffe junior had a servant named Joshua Wilson who, according to O'Rorke, cunningly got the upper hand of his good-for-nothing master. When Radcliffe died in 1679 he left his half-share equally between an aunt, Margaret Trappes, and Wilson. Mrs. Trappes sold her share to a Dr. John Leslie. In 1687 the three joint owners, namely Strafford, Wilson and Dr. Leslie divided the lands held jointly between them into three demarcated separate properties. On Wilson's death he left his holding to his daughter, who had married Sir Francis Leicester. It was this land which was bought from Sir Francis by Owen Wynne II in 1722.

CHAPTER EIGHT

Owen Wynne III
1686-1755

When Owen Wynne III succeeded his uncle in 1737 he was the first of the Wynnes to combine in one ownership the family lands in Counties Leitrim, Cavan and Sligo. He was born in about 1686. We have already seen from his petition quoted in chapter seven that as soon as he was able to serve the Crown, that is at the age of 19 or 20, he joined the army, bought a company two years later and served several years in Flanders. Burke states that he was educated at Trinity College, Dublin; if that is correct then he was probably at Trinity for a short time before starting his army service. He married his first cousin Catherine, daughter of Col. John Ffolliott of Donegal and his wife Lucy, daughter of Owen Wynne I. Owen III and Catherine had three sons, James, Owen (later Owen IV) and John, and two daughters, Lucy and Hannah. Hannah in 1743 married William Ormsby M.P. of Willowbrook (three miles from Sligo, on the road to Glencar). She thus became an ancestress of the Ormsby-Gore family.

Owen III was High Sheriff of County Sligo in 1723 and again in 1745, and he filled the same office in County Leitrim in 1724. He died at the age of 79 in 1755. His wife, Catherine died in 1778. When she was young she had been much concerned with her children's education. In January, 1737, she wrote from Dublin to Edward Martin, the Wynne agent in Sligo, a letter which, with the original spelling and punctuation unchanged, is as follows:-

> *"I am afraid my boys are not yet gone to school it gives*
> *me great concern that they have been so long at school and*
> *are so little the better and I am afraid they are not sencable*
> *of it themselves or they would be pressing to goe back to*

indeaver to improve themselves before they grow up great ignorant felows that will be ashamed when they don't know how to converce with gentlemen. I beg of you press this home to them and let them be sent to Raphoe immediately if they make three or four days journey insted of two, or more to walk half way it would not hurt them for every body can travel that has business of any importance and I am sure they have if they consider it. I hope Jack has larn'd to read Inglish if he ever intends to larn any thing, they both write and spell badly, my blessing to them and give them half guineys apiece for me. I have sent cloath to make them coat weastcoat and two pr of britches by Murphy but let them not wait for them but let Maginice keep their measure and let them be sent to them when they are ready with what other things they want Mrs. Martin can see and send them away as soon as possible. I hope you make the pigons and the swans to fed and that the deer in the parke and Jeny and Wooly are fed or they'l all dy I beg you'l enquire how Jeny Miles is or if you can spare her a little hay if she wants it for I am afraid she and her cattle will be starvd in that poor place and be soe kind to write to me and tell how you and Mrs. Martin have your health and answer what I write."

Owen junior, at least, very soon became literate. He went from Raphoe to a school at Longford. One of his letters home, written in a large childish but very legible hand, has survived. His spelling of the word 'cloaths' was the usual spelling at that time. The letter is as follows:

Dr Mama

I long very much to hear from you and to hear how my brother Jack's leg is. My cloaths are now very bad. I beg you may speak to my Dada to write to Mr. Neligan to buy me cloaths here. I beg you may send word when my brother Jack will come to Longford which is all from your dutiful son:

Owen Wynne.

My duty to my Dada and Uncle and love to my brothers and sisters.

41

Owen III's eldest son, James, died in 1748, eight years before his father's death. He was M.P. for County Sligo from 1737 to the time of his death. He married Susanna, eldest daughter and co-heiress of Sir Arthur Shaen, second and last baronet of Kilmore, County Roscommon, but they had no children. This marriage was hardly a success. O'Rorke refers to a lawsuit of 1745 where the Plantiff was Susanna Wynne and the defendant her husband, James Wynne. In this action Owen Wynne, James' father, swore an affidavit in which he stated that he and Susanna Wynne were travelling to Dublin in their coach when James Wynne and others came up to the coach at Drom0d, County Leitrim, cocked pistols at Owen and the coachman, and forced Susanna away, notwithstanding all her efforts and those of her father-in-law. He stated further that he believed Susanna's life to be in great danger. The outcome of the lawsuit is unfortunately unknown, but the episode suggests that if James had out-lived his father and inherited Hazelwood, the family's history might have been different. Fortunately, Susanna remarried after James' death and, we may hope, found happiness.

Owen Wynne III was a colonel in the army. In 1752 his son, later Owen IV, wished to buy a lieut-colonelcy of dragoons. At the time, and indeed until the 1870's, the middle commissioned ranks in the army were usually obtained by purchase, the purchase price being paid to the officer who was relinquishing the rank. To help his son in this endeavour Owen III wrote to Lord George Sackville, the brother and secretary of the Lord Lieutenant. Sackville in reply thought that the matter could be arranged, but because at the time Owen IV was but a captain, the King, George II, would have to be satisfied of his competence before he would sanction his promotion to colonel. Owen III sent on Sackville's letter to his son and pressed the latter to pursue the matter, adding that he believed the price to be £4,000. The system under which a commission could be purchased, though strongly defended in the next century by the Duke of Wellington, strikes the modern reader as extraordinary. Even more surprising is the price which had to be paid. The purchase of commissions was not abolished until 1871.

Towards the end of his life Owen III was prodded into founding a

Charter School in Sligo. He does not appear to have been over-enthusiastic for, when the decision was taken, the Bishop of Elphin wrote to him to say (after thanking him for a gift of venison) that he, the bishop, was glad that Wynne had at last resolved to get things going, as hitherto he had moved at a snail's pace. The Charter Schools were boarding schools to which were sent poor children found begging. The children were brought up as Protestants and were given a very indifferent education. The system collapsed in about 1825. The school in Sligo occupied a site close to where Calry Church was to be built. In 1862 the Elphin Dioccesan school was transferred to the old Charter School building and became the forerunner of the present Grammar School.

By the middle of the 18th century the merchants of Sligo were becoming restive over the payment to the Wynne family of tolls and customs on goods brought into the town for sale. In particular a Thomas Jones of Ardnaglass wanted to see the 'patent' under which such rights had been granted. Edward Martin, the agent, wrote to Wynne at his home in Abbey Street, Dublin, telling him what was happening. Jones had sent into Sligo three barrels of wheat to a baker and a hide to a tanner, but he did this on a day which was not a market day. The customs men had seized these goods and had lodged them in the market house until the next market day. Jones swore that he would lay out hundreds of pounds to get the country eased of such a burden. Further, a John King had sent three sacks of malt to his own house in the town, intending to sell the malt from there to the town's brewers. The sacks, which were sent in by night, were seized by the customs men but were repossessed by force by the King family. More trouble of a similar kind lay in the years ahead.

Owen III's third son, John, the 'Jack' referred to in young Owen's letter, was M.P. for Sligo from 1751 to 1760 and again from 1769 to 1778 and for County Leitrim from 1761 to 1778. He died unmarried.

Owen III died in 1755 and was succeeded by his second son, Owen IV.

43

CHAPTER NINE

The Right Honourable Owen Wynne IV
Died 1789

In 1754, before he inherited the family estates, Owen Wynne IV married Anne Maxwell whose brother, John, the M.P. for County Cavan, was created Baron Farnham in the Irish peerage in 1756. The Maxwell family had reached Ireland from Scotland in the reign of Elizabeth. By co-incidence Anne's grandfather had been Bishop of Kilmore in 1643. That bishopric was abolished during the Commonwealth. Following the Restoration he was bishop of the combined sees of Kilmore and Ardagh. These are the two sees in which Owen Wynne I in 1658 had, during the Commonwealth, obtained his profitable bishops' leases.

Owen IV was elected in 1749 M.P. for County Sligo in the Irish Parliament. He became an Irish Privy Councillor in 1756; this gave him the title of Right Honourable. His house in Dubin was in Henrietta Street. This broad street, rising up to what would be the King's Inns, was built on a grand scale. Cassels, the architect of Hazelwood, was responsible for the design of some of the houses. While in Dublin Owen received a regular stream of letters from Edward Martin, his agent in Sligo. These letters, which extend in time from 1758 to 1766, throw much light on the life which revolved around Hazelwood. They refer to estate management, elections and the candidates in them, rents, the recovery and payment of debts, the employment of servants, the cutting of turf, and so on. Mrs. Martin was in charge of brewing; she pickled salmon in kegs of spice, wine and vinegar, while on one occasion 600 oysters were pickled. As required, kegs were sent to the Wynne household in Dublin. An ice house was constructed, work which required digging to a depth of twenty feet. In 1764 a domestic crisis blew up when a housemaid named Molly Fleming was found to be pregnant, the father being another servant named Johnston. Molly was discharged and Johnston forgiven. Of Molly, Martin wrote: "I am really sorry for her and I believe her otherwise to be a good servant". As to Johnston, Martin naively commented: "He promises fair he never will be guilty of the like again". The episode is an example of the widely-held view that it is always the woman's fault.

Some pages of Martin's ledger relating to disbursements survive. The entries cover the years from 1758 to 1761 and contain dozens of headings relating to the functioning of an agricultural estate. More personal entries relate to the purchase of brandy and wine. In the three year period there is only one entry relating to port; on that occasion eight dozen bottles were bought. Apart from claret, wines such as hock were bought at a rate of a dozen bottles at a time. During the period three hogsheads (46 gallons each) of claret were bought from a wine merchant in Derry. When Owen was High Sheriff of County Sligo in 1758 he paid for such items as the entertainment of the judges, the provision of trumpeters and halberdiers and the transport of felons to Dublin. As is shown in a receipted bill of 1785 he paid a total of £23 to a Dublin boat builder for a 20 foot boat, together with its masts, sails, rigging and oars. This boat was transported by road to Lough Gill.

Systematic afforestation was carried out on the Wynne estate and on other lands taken on long leases for the purpose. By an Act of the Irish Parliament of 1783/84 a financial advantage was offered for the planting of trees, and for this purpose the landowner had to make annually a sworn return stating the varieties and numbers of trees planted during the previous twelve months. The record of these returns extends in time from 1785 to 1835 and thus relate to Owen IV and Owen V. During this fifty years period the number of trees planted is just short of 200,000. Twenty-three different varieties were included, the largest number being Scots fir, alder and ash, with oak and beech not far behind.

Owen IV died in 1789 leaving six sons and three daughters. His eldest son, Owen, succeeded to the family estates. The next son, John, died unmarried while the other sons, Henry, Robert, Richard and William founded families of their own, thus accounting for the extended family of Wynne who survive and thrive to the present day. There were in addition three daughters, Elizabeth, Judith and Catherine.

CHAPTER TEN

Owen Wynne V
1755-1841

Owen Wynne V was born in 1755 and died aged 86 in 1841. He was twice High Sheriff of County Sligo during his father's lifetime. A year after he succeeded to the family estates he married Lady Sarah Elizabeth Cole, the eldest daughter of the first Earl of Enniskillen. The family of Cole had originated in Ireland with Sir William Cole, an undertaker in the plantation of Ulster in the reign of James I. The family seat, Florence Court, built in the 1760's, lies seven miles from Enniskillen.

Owen V first entered the Irish Parliament in 1778 as member for County Sligo, while at the same time his father was member for the borough. Owen junior's opponent in the election was his father's brother-in-law, William Ormsby of Willowbrook. The contest was fought with a great deal of corruption and disorder on both sides, with the result that Owen's election was followed by a petition to unseat him. At the hearing of the petition by a committee of the Irish House of Commons, proceedings which lasted for two years, leading counsel for Wynne was John Philpot Curran, this being the first major case in which the great advocate took part. The committee heard evidence of bribery and evidence that the poll book was stolen and the electoral lists thrown in the river, and it is surprising to learn that instead of ordering a fresh election the committee upheld the election of Wynne. The costs of the hearing were so great that, according to O'Rorke, the effects were felt by both families after a lapse of a hundred years.

In subsequent elections, all of them expensive, Owen held one of the county seats until, on the death of his father, he returned himself for the borough seat which had been his father's. He retired from Parliament in 1806 by being appointed Escheator of Munster. This was purely a nominal post but, because it was an office of profit under the Crown, it disqualified its holder from membership of the Commons. It was a device by which a Member of Parliament could resign in between elections. Its modern equivalent in the U.K. is the office of Steward of the Chiltern Hundreds. He then 'sold' his borough seat to George Canning for an annuity which continued until 1820 when the seat was resumed by Owen.

It follows that Owen V was a member of the Irish House of Commons during the fateful debates at the end of the century concerning the union of the two Kingdoms. The Act of Union was finally passed by a majority of 67 votes. The fact that the measure could only be carried by the use of bribery and the wholesale distribution of titles and sinecure offices shows that the members, who were all Protestants, had serious doubts about the wisdom of the step. It was known on all sides that full Catholic emancipation would follow on the heels of the Act. This meant that if the Irish Parliament remained in being it would be swamped with Catholic members. But the passage of the Act, followed by a delay of nearly thirty years before full Catholic emancipaton was conceded, provided the root from which grew many of the unhappy differences between Britain and Ireland in the following two centuries. In the fulness of time the Act spelt the end of the Irish Protestant ascendancy. Owen voted against the bill, as also did the two county members, Edward Joshua Cooper and Charles O'Hara.

The growth of religious toleration from the reign of Elizabeth onwards had been a slow process. By 1800 freedom of worship and the right to vote and hold office had been extended to include Catholics and Dissenters, but Catholics still suffered from one serious disability. The right to sit in Parliament required the making of a declaration against transubstantiation. Thus after the Act of Union those Catholics in Ireland who were within the narrow limits of the franchise were still denied Catholic candidates for whom they could vote. The agitation for Catholic emancipation centred on this one disability. The Catholics of Great Britain were of course under the same disability, but since they were a small minority the issue there had not the same importance as in Ireland.

The Protestants of Ireland had no doubt what the consequences of emancipaton would be. A meeting of Protestants was held in the court house of Sligo on the 12th August, 1812. This meeting passed four resolutions, each proposed by Owen Wynne. The first declared that Catholic emancipation would involve a fundamental change in the religious and civil constitution of the United Kingdom. The second spoke of the trust which the Protestant gentry had in their Roman Catholic fellow-subjects and countrymen. But the substance of the matter is to be found in the third resolution:-

47

'Resolved, That it appears to us that the unqualified Repeal of these Laws would not be consistent with that perfect safety to the Constitution which we feel we have a right to require, but would eventually substitute in its place a Roman Catholic Ascendancy, which would proceed to a domination necessarily subversive to the Protestant settlement of the country on the preservation and strength of which, we firmly believe, the connection between the two countries, and ultimately the security of the Empire, to depend'.

The fourth resolution stated that, in the event of repeal or modification of the laws in question, provision must be made for the preservation of the constitution in church and state, and that all foreign interference in the nomination of Catholic clergy should be excluded. This meant that the Church of Ireland must not be disestablished and that the dreaded influence of the Papacy must be excluded as far as possible.

As a result of the meeting of August 1812, an *'Address to the Protestant Inhabitants of the Town and County of Sligo'* was published. In this a change in the attitude of Catholics was noted: "what was petition is now claim, what was prayed for as a boon is now demanded as a right". Two results would flow from a change in the law. First, "it must lead eventually to Roman Catholic domination. The disproportion of our numbers makes this danger more alarming". Secondly, it would lead eventually to the separation of England and Ireland: "Separation the object, our downfall the means, Roman Catholic agitation the instrumentality by which this is sought to be accomplished".

The Catholic Emancipation Act of 1829 substituted for the declaration against transubstantiation an inoffensive oath of allegiance to the Crown, thus enabling Catholics to sit in the House of Commons. Subsequent history has shown how accurately Wynne and his fellow Protestants foresaw the future. If a Catholic had foreseen the future in the same light, to him such developments would have appeared as no more than justice which for too long had been delayed.

During the 18th century Ireland was stripped of regular troops since the army was employed abroad, particularly in fighting the colonists in the American War of Independence. Taking advantage of England's difficulties, France and Spain entered that war on the side of the colonists, thereby raising the spectre of invasion. To meet such threats public-spirited Irishmen, led by the landlords, formed volunteer corps. The equipment, such as it was, had to be provided by the officers themselves, and all the volunteers were unpaid. Even the uniforms were provided by the commanding officer. Wynne raised and commanded the Sligo Volunteers.The volunteers developed into political associations demanding legislative and commercial independence for Ireland as a separate (Protestant) nation under the reigning monarch as King of Ireland. Volunteer conventions were held to demand parliamentary reform, the best known being that at Dungannon in 1782. Immediately following Dungannon a Connaught convention was held at Ballinasloe, the delegates from Co. Sligo being significantly the Protestant landowners Colonels O'Hara, Gore, Irwin and Ormsby. The proposals made by these conventions were rejected by the Irish Parliament. When the volunteer movement was overtaken by the United Irishmen, founded in 1791 first in Belfast and then in Dublin, the government was faced with a serious problem which led to the suppression of the volunteers and the establishment in 1795 by Act of Parliament of an Irish militia. In the militia regiments which were then formed the officers received their commissions from the Crown, and the troops when embodied were paid by the Crown. These steps were rendered necessary by the prospect, all too soon fulfilled, of a long-drawn out war with revolutionary France. Wynne, with the rank of captain, commanded the Carbury Cavalry, a unit which was raised in 1791. In the following year he was commissioned also as captain of the County Sligo Light Infantry. This unit was stationed in the south of Ireland and distinguished itself at Vinegar Hill, Wexford, in June 1798, where the 'rebels' were defeated.

On the 22nd August, 1798, the French General Humbert, with about 1,000 experienced French troops, landed at Killala. When the French reached Collooney their numbers had been increased by deserters from some County Mayo militia regiments and by a large and very ill-armed body of Irish 'rebels'. The principal force which engaged the French at the Battle of Carrignagat, where the statue of Captain Teeling now stands, was the City of Limerick Regiment of Militia under Col. Vereker. This unit, which was stationed in Sligo, consisted chiefly of 'the Garryowen Boys'. A Capt. Harley writng in 1838 described them as "a fearless race of men from the south side of Limerick who, before their enlistment, spent most of their time in drinking and fighting but after being embodied suffered a remarkable metamorphosis into the smartest, best disciplined and also the most wicked regiment in Ireland". These troops deflected Humbert from entering Sligo and they taught the French that the Irish militia, if trained and armed, was a formidable force. At Ballinamuck, County Longford, a fortnight later the French were defeated by the Down, Armagh and Kerry Militias.

There remained Killala, still held by the French together with large numbers of Irishmen. The town was attacked from two directions, Sligo and Ballina. Amongst the troops advancing from Ballina were Captain O'Hara's Captain Wynne's and Captain Crofton's yeomanry regiments. Since the defeat of their main army at Ballinamuck, the French at Killala were anxious to surrender, but the Irish decided to continue the fight. They fought with pikes and a few muskets from behind low stone walls until, within the space of an hour, four hundred were killed. It has been said that their courage would have gone down in history had their decision to fight been taken by an authorized army of any nation. Then followed the reprisals, the burning of cabins and the hunting down of fugitives. Dr. Stock, the Protestant bishop, who had been in Killala throughout the French experience, condemned the behaviour of the government troops. But these troops were out of control of their officers. To quote the bishop: "Their rapacity differed in no respect from that of the rebels except that his Majesty's soldiers were incomparably superior to the Irish traitors in dexterity at stealing".

Two contemporary writers commented on Owen Wynne V's merits or demerits as a landlord. E. Wakefield, whose 'Ireland, Statistical and Political' was published in 1812, is fulsome in his praise:

"If a high and dignified sense of honour; inflexible integrity; close application to business; an ardent zeal for the interest of one's native country, displayed in cultivating its soil, and improving its inhabitants, can create esteem and respect, then ought this gentleman to have a seat in Parliament, where the assistance of his talents and experience, at this perilous time, might be of essential service. As a great landed proprietor he spreads civilisation around him by residing on his estate and spending a princely income among his tenants; as a father in the bosom of a numerous and happy family, who respect and adore him, he sets an example which cannot fail of having a beneficial influence on his servants, neighbours and dependants; as a magistrate, discharging the duties of that important office, with strict attention to impartial justice, he is enabled to repress disorder, and to maintain peace and tranquillity".

Nobody can be quite so perfect as this, nor can the world around one be quire so perfect either. H.D. Inglis, who wrote 'A Journey Throughout Ireland in 1834', is more critical. Inglis writes:

"The land in the barony of Carbury, especially Mr. Wynne's is let extremely high. Mr. Wynne's tenants are, with very few exceptions, in

50

arrear, but he is one of those short-sighted landlords who is resolved at all costs to keep up the nominal amount of his rent-roll. His rents are taken in dribbles, in shillings and copper; and agents have been known to accompany tenants to market with their produce, lest any part of its value should escape the landlords' pocket. This gentleman has been at great pains to establish a Protestant tenancy on his estate".

Inglis, however, was highly critical of all Irish landlords whom he described as sordid, avaricious and oppressive. He further accused them of a heartless desertion of their country. Such words might be justifiable in the case of absentee landlords, but at no time were the Wynnes absentees. Nor were they lacking in their concern for the welfare of their tenants. In commenting on Inglis, O'Rorke says that it would hardly be denied that the owners of the Hazelwood estate had been exceptionally sectarian in the selection of tenants. Yet a glimmer of light pierces the gloom of sectarianism when we learn that in 1831 Owen Wynne made a free gift of an acre of land to the parish priest of Ballaghmeehan, Co. Leitrim, for the purpose of building a church. In the same year he let land at a peppercorn rent to the rector and churchwarden of Drumcliff for the building of a Protestant school. The rector at the time was John Yeats, to whom W.B. Yeats refers in *'Under Benbulben': 'An ancestor was rector there long years ago'*.

But above all Owen V was a notable agricultural pioneer, intent on bringing the benefits of the English agrarian revolution to Ireland. When the young Palmerston, inheritor of land in Dublin and north-west County Sligo, paid his first visit to Ireland in 1808, he wrote a letter to his sister in which he said:

"Mr. Wynne is an excellent country gentleman and just the sort of person of whom could one put down one every thirty miles throughout Ireland it would in forty years time become as much civilised as England".

In 1802 James McParlan published for the Dublin Society his *'Statistical Survey of the County of Sligo'*. Perhaps surprisingly he described the whole county as tillage country; together with Mayo it was the principal granary and supplier of potatoes for the manufacturing counties of the north in times of scarcity. He states that an immense quantity of oats, barley and potatoes was grown, together with some wheat following the potatoes. He himself qualifies this generalisation by pointing out that a third of the county was bog and waste land, while tillage was mostly confined to the baronies of Tireragh along the north-west coast of the county, Corran, centred on Ballymote, and Carbury. Sligo was said to be the best port in Ireland for the export of grain, particularly oats, to all parts of the Irish coast and also to Britain. The growing of crops was a fairly recent development, the land having been used only as sheep-walks a quarter of a century earlier. The export of grain was stimulated by the Napoleonic wars. These factors made improvements to the plough of signal importance. The old Irish plough, sometimes tied to the horse's tail, had left half of the surface unturned. Wynne experimented with different kinds of plough, in 1801 winning a prize at Ballinasloe for one of his designs. McParlan saw six ploughs at work one morning at Hazel-wood; one was a double plough drawn by three horses, four were each drawn by two oxen, and one was drawn by one horse. To McParlan the quantity of work done in one morning was astonishing. He was particularly impressed by two-wheeled ploughs each drawn by a pair of oxen and managed by one man who, by means of long reins connected to bridle-bits in the oxen's mouths, guided them with the same ease as horses.

An advertisement of 1805 sets out the prizes offered by Wynne to his tenants in Sligo and Leitirm. The first prizes are sums of up to £2–5–6. Prizes were to be awarded for the following:- the farm in the best condition and the best state of cultivation (the state of the fences being particularly important); the farmer who shall plough the greatest acreage with one man and two horses driven by reins without a leader; the farmer who shall have the best crop of, respectively, potatoes cultivated with the plough, turnips, and red clover; the farmer who shall have planted the greatest number of forest trees, not less than three hundred; the wife or widow of a labourer who shall have spun the greatest quantity of flax in the year, or knitted the greatest number of pairs of stockings; and the labourer who shall have his house, garden and children in the neatest, cleanest and most decent order. To this last category the following conditions were added:- he must have white–washed his house at least once in the year, inside and outside, must have a paved or gravelled way in front of his house free from dung and dirt, and must not have admitted his cow or pig into his dwelling house on any account whatsoever.

Two fifths of the habitations throughout Ireland consisted of so-called cabins. These have often been described, and it is plain that they were mostly little more than hovels. But on landlords' estates the tenants' housing often consisted of two–roomed cottages. Wynne tried to do better than that. Just outside the boundary of the demesne, he built twelve new cottages each of which consisted of four rooms with a small work room at the back. These, or at least some of them, can still be seen and they can readily be identified by the fact that the sloping roof at the rear continues further towards the ground than the roof at the front. They are still sometimes referred to as 'the golden rappers', for when they were built they represented such an advance in amenities and comfort that they were said to deserve golden rappers (door knockers) on the front doors. Alternatively they were 'golden wrappers' because the tenants were metaphorically wrapped in gold. The cottages, which are semi–detached, stood on units of three acres, which was about the average holding in the county at the time. The rent for each cottage was at the somewhat high figure of £5 annually.

As regards stock, Wynne introduced Devon cattle and South Down sheep from England. In correspondence with his brother Richard, Owen stated that the Farming Society of Ireland was prepared to buy £400 worth of Merino rams and ewes and resell them at the market at Balli-nasloe. He planted shrubs, perennials and rockplants in the gardens at Hazelwood and a list of these survives from 1805; even sub–species are recorded, sometimes as many as four or five. We have already seen that he continued his father's widespread afforestation. Much of this was carried out for commercial purposes. He made a calculation of the cost of and profit from an acre of larch, progressively felled at different heights over a period of twenty years. Where 17,640 trees were planted on an acre two feet apart the net profit over that period amounted to £1,420.

Hostility to the payment of tolls to the Wynne family on goods brought for sale to the market at Sligo continued and efforts were made to avoid such payment. The nature of what was going on may be judged from the instructions by Wynne's solicitor to counsel when he asked for the latter's opinion. In 1796 two merchants of Sligo bought a flour mill at Ballysadare. A number of men employed by these merchants induced persons passing through to bring their oats to the stores at Ballysadare. To make matters worse, these merchants themselves levied a toll of one stone of oats for every twenty–five stones brought to them. In the same year merchants in the town were inducing farmers to bring in grain on non–market days, followed by a refusal to pay toll. The result of these evasions was that the quantity and quality of grain for sale on market days had been reduced. In 1805 a miller of Sligo was buying grain in Roscommon, bringing it to the town on a non–market day, and then milling the flour without paying toll. This miller also imported grain by sea from Limerick. Counsel advised that the steps taken at Ballysadare constituted the offence of forestalling the market, while the other prac-tices, if deliberate, were actionable as fraud. This vexed question of the tolls was to reach its climax as the century advanced.

A wider range of complaints was directed against Owen Wynne in a petition of Thomas Flanagan on behalf of the inhabitants of Sligo addressed to both Houses of Parliament. It was presented and read in one and perhaps both Houses on the 10th May, 1819, and it was ordered that it should lie on the table, that is that no action should be taken on it. The petition was as follows:

"That a meeting of the merchants, traders and inhabitants of the town of Sligo in the Kingdom of Ireland was lately held in the Court House of Sligo in pursuance of a requisition for that purpose at which petitioner was Chairman, when it was unanimously resolved to petition both Houses of Parliament for redress of the grievances herein mentioned.

That the town of Sligo is of great extent, the population of which amounts to upwards of fifteen thousand inhabitants, and is one of the best trading towns in Ireland.

That it would be of the highest importance to have a Board of Aldermen or some other Board for the due management of the affairs of the town and for the improvement thereof, Freemen and a Guild of Merchants, and Sheriffs to be annual and elective, with a power of recovering debts under £10.

That the ancient charter authorized a Provost, Burgesses and a Guild of Merchants in Sligo to be of the commonalty of the town for the encouragement of commerce, trade and industry, which is not now the case.

That very large sums of money are levied in the town of Sligo for tolls and customs which by right ought to go to the improvement of the town but which sums are appropriated to private purposes and that large and excessive sums are levied under pretence of improving the town and yet the streets are scarce paved, no light at night nor watchmen for the protection of the property of the inhabitants and that the commonage of Sligo, the property of the inhabitants of the town, is become the assumed property of a private individual, and although the inhabitants of Sligo most cheerfully contribute to the public expenditure they are not only without those benefits and advantages but are without the benefit of the elective franchise.

May it therefore please your Lordships to grant unto the inhabitants of the town of Sligo their rights and privileges and to enact such

laws and regulations for the benefit of the inhabitants of the town as
to your Lordships in your wisdom and justice may seem reasonable".
  For the inhabitants of Sligo.
  Thomas Flanagan, Chairman of the Meeting.
  London, May 3rd, 1819.

Owen Wynne wrote to Sir Robert Peel on the subject of this petition.
In 1819 Peel was not in office, but he had been Chief Secretary for
Ireland from 1812 to 1818. He replied to Wynne by letter dated the 27th
December, 1819, in which he wrote:

*"I well know Mr Thomas Flanagan and that he is one of the most
impudent impostors that ever attempted to deceive the credulity of
others. He was constantly writing to me in Ireland, but I soon found
from his own account of himself that he was a contemptible wretch,
and took no notice of his letters. I recollect he forwarded me a com-
plimentary address from Sligo which he declared himself to be commissioned to transmit to me by a numerous meeting, he having forged
the address and the meeting never having existed anywhere but in his
own imagination. I took him for a strange compound of a rogue and
a madman.*

*I have no doubt that his petition made not the slightest impression. I
wish I had been in the House when it was brought up. I would have said
something with respect to it, even if I had not received your letter and had
not therefore an additional inducement to expose such an impostor.*

*Unless some notice is hereafter taken of it and some proceeding initi-
ated, I doubt the policy of alluding to it and of thus answering one object
that Mr. Flanagan has in view, that of being brought to notice.*

*I was aware that this fellow had been committed to prison for
some gross offence. I recollect too I have got the papers relating to it.
If my memory does not fail me, Judge Maguire tried him. I am sure I
am not responsible for the remission of his punishment".*

Whether or not Thomas Flanagan was an impostor and whether or not
the meeting to which he referred ever took place, the opinions that he
expressed were justified, not only as regards the Wynne family but also
in respect of comparable abuses throughout the Kingdom. In 1819, four
years after the end of the Napoleonic wars, Parliament was fearful of
reform, but popular opinion was increasingly demanding it. In the very
same year as that in which Flanagan presented his petition the so-called
Massacre of Peterloo took place in Manchester, when a crowd of some

60,000 spinners and weavers demanding the right to vote was dispersed by cavalry charges. Reform could not long be delayed. The first steps towards establishing something resembling parliamentary and then municipal democracy were taken in the 1830's. Later in the century the anomaly of charging tolls on goods brought for sale to the market at Sligo with the profits finding their way into private hands, was abolished. These matters are dealt with in chapter thirteen under the title 'Wynne Power Dismantled'.

An amusing light is thrown on the religious and social divisions in Sligo by a controversy which arose in the autumn of 1819 over a play which was presented at the town theatre. At that time the theatre was situated in part of the Linenhall, the building which runs from the Imperial Hotel along what is now called John F. Kennedy Parade and which is characterised by a series of round arched windows. The first rumblings of this storm in a teacup began when Mr. Clarke, a travelling actor and producer of plays, presented *The Beggars' Opera*. It was the practice at the time, as Clarke later said by way of explanation, to interpolate into a play a mention of the name of any person known in the town as an improper character. Such an interpolation was made in the Sligo production of *The Beggars' Opera*. History does not relate what the precise words were; all that Clarke would admit to was that one of the players interposed the line; "I would have brought Biddy Feeny here, but she was not at home". Whatever significance this phrase might have had, it is probable that the words uttered went rather further. For they provoked an angry reaction from the Rev. W.C. Armstrong, the Provost, who was also a magistrate and the respected master of a Protestant classical school.

Mr. Armstrong had formed a society for ameliorating the condition of unfortunate females confined in the town prison. This society had already encountered much ridicule when, to quote Armstrong, it was most indecently slandered on the stage of the Sligo theatre in the production of *The Beggars' Opera*. Armstrong repeated his view at a meeting of the Society for Disseminating the Holy Scriptures. The probability is that the interpolation in the play suggested that the prison visitors did not always confine their interest to spiritual matters.

Mr. Clarke, who was particularly incensed because Mr. Armstrong referred to him as an itinerant player, did not let the matter rest. In a playbill he announced that on Friday the 24th September, 1819, a performance of a much admired comedy called *The Hypocrite* would be staged at the theatre. The playbill made the comment: "It is a valuable trait of this comedy that it carefully distinguishes between rational piety

56

and hypocrisy, fanaticism and outrageous pretensions to sanctity which it so severely satirises".

On reading this playbill Armstrong was incensed for he regarded the comment as directed against himself. He forbade the presentation of the play, but Clarke made it clear that he intended to go on. On the morning of the day of the performance Armstrong distributed a handbill addressed to the inhabitants of Sligo in which he reviewed his version of the facts and wrote: "Understanding that the Theatre will be opened on the evening of this day in direct opposition to me, and therefore illegally, I take this opportunity of expressing my hope that a measure so subversive of good order and good government will not be supported by the presence of any of those I have the honour to address". He also wrote to Owen Wynne, requesting that Clarke should be arrested, describing the theatre as a rallying point for the turbulent and disaffected, which, he said, was itself a sufficient cause for magisterial interference. Clarke appears to have faltered in the face of Armstrong's wrath, for he postponed the presentation of the play until Monday, the 27th September. However, produced it was. Armstrong was given an account of it and passed on his information by letter to Wynne. The play, he said, had passed off quietly, as all were on their best behaviour. The only ladies present (meaning Protestants) were Mrs. Abraham Fenton, two Miss Kellys and Mrs. Coyne. The gentlemen present (meaning Protestants) were Mr. Abraham Fenton (the Coroner), Mr. Barklie, Mr. Workman, Everard Scott and Mr. Vincent who played the piano to Miss Kelly's singing. None of the military attended. The house was filled with Roman Catholics of the town.

The production of 'The Hypocrite' was Mr. Clarke's benefit night and Armstrong heard that he was to have another benefit. Armstrong wrote again to Wynne advising that should Clarke advertise another play his arrest would be necessary as such contempt of civil authority must be dangerous to society.

Armstrong wrote to his bishop and Wynne wrote to the Lord Lieutenant. A reply, dated the 5th October, was received from Dublin Castle. After agreeing with Wynne's opinion of the importance and necessity of repressing all attacks upon religion and all opposition to the established authorities, the letter continued:

"In the present case, however, it does not appear that the Government can interfere to prevent Mr. Clarke continuing his theatricals. It seems there is no law which makes the permission of the magistrate necessary for such exhibitions. In so far then as relates to the mere circumstance of having plays against the desire of the Provost, the

Government is not legally empowered to interfere. If there be committed any breach of public morals or decency, that may of course be animadverted upon by the magistrate, and is within his jurisdiction, but that is a different question from the present".

When this letter was received and shown to Armstrong, Armstrong wrote to Wynne regretting the state of the law and suggesting it should be changed. In this letter he told Wynne that Clarke had written to him a farewell letter threatening to take action against Armstrong, presumably for referring to him in the handbill as an itinerant player. But by this time the waves in the teacup were subsiding and no more was heard of the matter.

It is worth noting that in one of his letters to Wynne on the subject of the play Armstrong wrote:-

"Mr. Martin never stood on worse ground than he does at present and I can assure you your advising a strong measure at this juncture will most materially strengthen your interest in Sligo and dismember the party hitherto opposed to you".

This is a reference to the enmity which existed between the Wynnes of Hazelwood and the Martin (later Wood–Martin) family of Cleveragh. There is some reason to think that Edward Martin, to whom Armstrong refers, challenged in the courts Wynne's right to the tolls and customs of the market and that Martin lost, being left with a heavy liability for costs.

As a member at Westminster Owen must have made fairly frequent crossings of the Irish sea. His other travels included a visit to Calais and Boulogne in 1824, accompanied by his wife, two sons, two daughters and Miss Whicker, his secretary, together with three 'domestics' and two servants. In November of the same year he travelled from Dublin to Bath. An account was kept of the expense of the four day journey. These totalled £66. The party consisted of nine persons, four being servants. The servants were a driver, two footmen and a man to handle the luggage. The coach and horses were slung on board ship at Dublin for the crossing to Holyhead.

These matters are relatively trivial; far more important was the recurring incidence of famine. In 1822 the potato crop failed and the production of oats fell. Some light is thrown on the situation in Sligo by reports sent by a local committee, of which Wynne was the chairman, to the Committee for the Relief of Distressed Districts in Ireland, a body known as the London Tavern Committee. Substantial sums were sent from London; by August, through contributions from London and from Sligo itself, the Sligo committee had £1,890 in hand. It was proposed to use £1,000 of this sum in the making of footpaths (not roads, which were the responsibility of government engineers) and to distribute the rest among widows and orphans. Famine was inevitably followed by cholera and dysentery. The Fever Hospital, which had just been built at the expense of the Cooper family of Markree, was soon over–crowded. The agent for the Sligo committee wrote to London to say that it would be better to encourage the declining spinning and weaving in the town rather than to send over clothes. It is probable that Owen's lead in improving the standard of his tenants' agriculture and stockbreeding was of some assistance outside the town; at least he had helped to diversify agriculture away from the potato.

For some years around 1800 Owen and two of his brothers, Henry and Richard, both clergymen in Ireland, sought to discover particulars of their Welsh ancestry. Henry noted the inscriptions on the Wynn tombs in the Gwydir chapel in Llanrwst church, but Richard was the moving spirit. The enquiry was largely prompted by the fallacious belief that Owen might be entitled to the then extinct baronetcy of Gwydir.

Richard corresponded with the Lloyds of Rhiwaedog, whose family had bought the Plas-yn-dre estate from James Wynne in 1681; with Joseph Williams, an eccentric living in London and a descendant of the family of Gwydir, who had served for years as a soldier in Ireland and who was waging a private war with a set of infamous lawyers who he said had defrauded him; and with a J. Pulman, an amateur researcher in the Herald's College in London.

Lloyd of Rhiwaedog, who claimed (probably correctly) that his family was descended from Rhirid Flaidd, pointed out the connection between Lewis Gwynne of Bala and the Wynns of Maesmochnant. He told Richard that he (Lloyd) had found in the British Museum a manuscript of about 1680 which set out correctly the ancestry of the Wynnes of Lurganboy back to Howell, fifth in descent from Rhirid Flaidd. Through Lloyd's help Richard himself discovered the will, dated 1527, of David ap Meredith. On the back of it were the following words written by Owen Wynne I. "This is the last will and testament of David ap Meredith ap Howell, my great-grandfather, whose heir I am, Owen Wynne, Bala, 5th June, 1665."

In the course of the correspondence Lloyd made this comment to Richard:

> *"It is some surprise to me that so respectable and opulent a family as yours have not ranked among the peers. I believe I recollect your father (Owen IV). He was not a courtier and the barter of titles for*

dependancy may not be acceptable to your brother's principles. That may account for his remaining with the Petit Gens".

Pulman was the most informative and accurate of the correspondents. He pointed out that the descent from Rhirid Flaidd on the one hand and from the Gwydir family and so back to Owen Gwynedd on the other hand were quite separate matters and that any claim to the Gwydir baronetcy was unfounded. In the end Richard, while anxious to establish a relationship with the Wynns of Gwydir, accepted that the direct descent was from Rhirid Flaidd. He noted correctly that Flaidd meant wolf and that that fact might account for the three wolves' heads on the coat of arms of the Irish Wynnes.

In one of these letters written by Owen to Richard from London, Owen remarked: "I wish you and Bob (another brother) would do your utmost to get me a cook – I don't know what I shall do on my return". This lack of a cook may relate to what Dr. Patrick Heraughty says in his book *'Innishmurray'*. Dr. Heraughty, who was born on Inishmurray, writes:

"At the beginning of the 19th century Inishmurray was almost deserted. And the owner of the estate sought the help of Owen Wynne of Hazelwood to solve the problem. He (Wynne) was a remarkable man who has scarcely been given due recognition for the social and agricultural advances for which he was responsible. He was a dedicated farmer; the proper and beneficial use of the land meant more to him than anything. He used nine different types of plough on his own land and received first prize at Ballinasloe Fair in 1810 for a plough designed by himself. It is not surprising that his advice was sought by neighbouring estates. He solved the problem of the depopulation of Inishmurray in the following way. Tadhg O'Heraughty, a tenant of Gore Booth, farmed a reasonably sized holding in Ballyconnell, Maugherow. Owen Wynne approached his heir, Domhnall O'Heraughty, with the proposition that in exchange for his land in Ballyconnell he take the whole of Inishmurray. Domhnall was not a ready taker and tried to parry the offer as best he could but both men knew that as a tenant Domhnall was in the weaker position. One of Domhnall's objections was that he would not be able to find a wife to live in isolation on the island. But the adroit Wynne was prepared for this and had obtained the consent of Margaret McNulty, a cook at Hazelwood, to marry Domhnall and go to the island with him. With this and some minor objections overcome, Domhnall had little choice but to accept the offer of Inishmurray".

CHAPTER ELEVEN

The Right Honourable John Arthur Wynne
1801 – 1865

John Arthur Wynne, born in 1801, was educated at Winchester and Christ Church, Oxford. He succeeded to the family estates in 1841 on the death of his father, Owen Wynne V. During his father's lifetime he had been High Sheriff of County Leitrim in 1834 and of County Sligo in 1840. In 1838 he married Lady Anne Butler, second daughter of the first Marquess of Ormonde.

Lady Anne's forebears were indeed distinguished in the history of Ireland. When Henry II visited Ireland in 1171 he conferred the chief Butlerage on Theobald Fitzwalter. Thereafter the Butlers, whether as Earls, Dukes or Marquesses of Ormonde played a dominant part in Irish affairs from their stronghold at Kilkenny Castle. The 'Great Duke' was Lord Lieutenant under both Charles I and Charles II; he strove to maintain the interests of the Crown against Irish rebels and English parliamentarians alike. He was the only actor to remain at the centre of the stage through fifty of the most turbulent years in Irish history. Lady Anne was clearly a young lady of charm and accomplishments. We obtain a glimpse of her from a letter written to her from Rome in the year of her marriage by a German artist named A. Kestner, who had been her art master at Kilkenny Castle:

"I am sure you have the most complete conviction that any fortunate event which happens to you or to any individual of your family makes me happy too, and very much happy. You may then measure my feelings when I was informed by Mrs. Coningham that you are a bride. I am sending you herein a little branch of myrtle which I pray you to twist in your bride–wreath. Were I nearer to you I would give you a better present. It is in the innocence of your heart that I think

THE RIGHT HONOURABLE
JOHN ARTHUR WYNNE

LADY ANNE WYNNE

you will accept this trifle from me equally smiling if it were a
diamond. I received some day in the collosseum–gardens a common
acacia–leaf in sign of affection from a child with whom I had played
there. Were you here I would try to make your portrait for Mr. Wynn.

Very often I remember the agreeable walks made with you, and
the comfortable evenings in your house, and singing and drawing,
and I was very sorry when the pleasure was over and your house was
void.

I pray you to remember me the most kindly to Lord and Lady
Ormonde and your sisters and brothers whose kindness I shall never
forget. I should be very much gratified when you would tell me the
name of the place where you go; and give me a description how it is".

The common acacia leaf given by the child to the writer is still
attached by a blob of sealing wax inside the fold of the letter. Lady Anne
died eleven years after her marriage, having borne four children.

In 1830 John Wynne succeeded his father as member of Parliament
for the Borough. This was by his father's nomination rather than by election, and it was the last occasion on which such a system could operate.
For the Reform Act of 1832 abolished the close or 'rotten' boroughs. Fol-

lowing the passing of the Act an election took place, albeit on a very restricted franchise, but in it Wynne was defeated by John Martin. John Martin was the choice of an anti-Wynne faction led by his father the redoubtable Abraham Martin, the owner of a distillery (George IV thought highly of his whiskey), a flour mill, bakery and the fishing in the Garavogue. Martin's appearance and manner, says O'Rorke, proclaimed that he was as much at home in the streets of Sligo as was the owner of the Borough, Owen Wynne, with whom he was often in conflict and at law. The election of his son was a great triumph for Abraham Martin, who secured it largely through enlisting the aid of the Parish Priest, Dean Donlevy, for the Wynnes, either by themselves or their nominees, had represented the Borough for a hundred and thirty years. Young Martin survived until 1837 when Dean Donlevy, dissatisfied with his performance in the House, put forward John Patrick Somers as his protegé. Somers, backed also by O'Connell who was then conducting his repeal movement, won the seat from Martin.

In 1843 John Wynne was appointed a member of the Devon Commission. This commission, under the chairmanship of the Earl of Devon, was set up by Sir Robert Peel to examine how far the Irish land system was responsible for the prevailing discontent and disturbance and how far Parliament should interfere. Of the five commissioners four were Irish landlords and the chairman was an Englishman who owned property in Ireland. This prompted O'Connell's comment that it would be as reasonable to consult butchers about the lenten fast as to consult landlords about the rights of tenants. After sitting for two years the commission failed to recommend the reforms later called the 'three F's', namely fair rent, fixity of tenure and freedom for the tenant to sell his interest in the holding. It did propose a limited right to compensation for improvement, but a bill to this effect was defeated in the House of Lords. On the other hand the report of the commission was no mere whitewash. It stated that the principal cause of Irish misery lay in the bad relations between landlord and tenant. Ireland was a conquered country, the Irish peasantry was dispossessed, and the landlords alien conquerors. By contrast, the equivalent relationship in England at its best did not have its roots in conquest but had evolved from feudalism into a hereditary paternalism. The report expressed the opinion that the superior prosperity and tranquillity of Ulster at that time, compared with the rest of Ireland, was due to the Ulster custom of tenant right by which compensation was paid by the landlord to the tenant for improvements made by the tenant. The condition of the people was described in the following words:

"It would be impossible adequately to describe the privations which the Irish labourer and his family habitually and silently endure. In many districts their only food is the potato, their only beverage water. Their cabins are seldom a protection against the weather; a bed or blanket is a rare luxury. A pig and a manure heap constitute their only property".

Those who read the report found in it nought for their comfort.

In 1843, as famine became more severe, John Wynne reduced his rents thereby lowering his annual income by £1,280. In the following year he applied to the Office of Public Works for a grant to improve the navigable channel to the port of Sligo. The application was refused on the ground that the Public Works Acts applied only to the piers and quays of a harbour and not to its channel. Nevertheless work on deepening the channel and making it more direct was undertaken by means of local subscriptions. In 1845 the Major of Sligo wrote to Wynne:

"The gentry and the landed propietors, as also the merchants of the town, have subscribed about £1,500 for the purpose of deepening the port and harbour. You were one of the principal subscribers. For the last 30 years we have not got a pound from the Government by way of a grant or loan".

After saying that a seventh part of the population of the town was unemployed the Mayor continued:

"They are not prone to drinking and are not indolent, but they are willing to do anything rather than seek relief in the Poorhouse, as you know from your constant attendance there".

But even then the Poorhouse contained more than 1,200 persons. Local subscriptions provided soup kitchens, the Government adding pound for pound to what was collected.

Like other landlords Wynne paid for the passage of emigrants. The accounts that survive, which may not be complete, show that he paid to Middleton and Pollexfen £364 for 81 passages. This figure represents more than 81 persons, for children counted as half a passage. A typical family group of two parents with children cost between £13 and £14 depending on the ship. On a similar basis, he paid £126–15–0 to Peter O'Connor. The destination in each case was Quebec. Of necessity he waived any claim for arrears of rent owed by any tenant who emigrated.

Arrears of rent inevitably increased. From Wynne's accounts for the years 1846 and 1847 one can extract the following round figures:-

	September 1846	March 1847
Accumulated arrears	3,000	4,000
Rent due	6,000	6,000
Total due	9,000	10,000
Rent received	5,000	6,500
Arrears	£4,000	£3,500

Much blame had been placed on the British Treasury for exacerbating the famine by adopting the economics of the free market, but that was the policy of all European states in similar circumstances. It was the policy adopted by the Irish themselves when they could. The Mayor in the letter quoted above says that food prices were high because the failure of the potato crop caused farmers to hold back their grain crop; the export of cattle to Liverpool and Glasgow also increased because of the higher prices there obtainable, aided by the introduction of steamships.

Meanwhile the growing industrialisation of England required a policy of cheap food. After much agitation by the Anti–Corn Law League, Sir Robert Peel in 1846 repealed the Corn laws. This step split the Conservative party, the representative of the landed interest, and gave the Whigs a nearly unbroken twenty years of office. A brief Conservative ministry under Lord Derby and Disraeli held office in 1852. In this ministry the Earl of Eglinton and Wilton was appointed Lord Lieutenant of Ireland. Lord Eglinton was best known for the Eglinton Tournament of 1839, a vast recreation of medievalism, at his castle in Scotland. On his appointment he wrote to Wynne:

> "I have been commissioned by Lord Derby to place at your disposal the office of Under Secretary for Ireland, which I trust you will favour me also by accepting".

Wynne accepted, thereby becoming the administrative head of the Irish civil service. In the following year he was appointed a Privy Councillor. His official residence in Dublin was the house in Phoenix Park which was used until recently as the residence of the Papal Nuncio. The Lord Lieutenant occupied what is now Aras an Uachtarain, while the Chief Secretary, when in Ireland, occupied the adjacent house which is now the house of the American Ambassador.

Lord Eglinton made himself an exceedingly popular Viceroy among those who were invited to Dublin Castle and he kept up the vice–regal court in princely style. Unfortunately all this was short–lived for the ministry fell within the year. After its fall Eglinton wrote to Wynne a letter which reflects the difficulties which the newly–formed Whig administration found in its attempts to deal with Irish problems. The matters referred to have faded into the past, unless some modern Irish historian is acquainted with the details. The letter, which is dated the 21st February, 1853, reads:

"The Irish Government seem not to have decided what they are to do with the Six Mile Bridge affair, but I have no doubt it will end in the prosecution both of the soldiers and the priests being abandoned, on the same principle that they balanced the proposed re–instatement of Lord Roden with that of Kirwan. I confess I think the latter was a most unwarrantable step, taken hastily and offensively and I mean to move for all the papers and correspondence connected with the case as soon as I get to London, with a view to commenting on it afterwards. They can hardly refuse them to me, but if they do I think with the help of your recollection and that of Balfour, as well as the ex-Chancellor, we can get up a good case.

What extraordinary indiscretion Graham and Wood have been guilty of, and how splendidly Dizzy (Disraeli) has shown them up. These old hands can get into scrapes quite as readily as us green-horns.

I have been enjoying my idleness with great relish and the frost has added considerably to my amusement. I have been curling on the sea every day for the last fortnight. I hope you do not find your time hang heavy on your hands, though I cannot help hoping that you rather regret the termination of our political connexion".

As a responsible landlord and as a one time member of the Devon Commission, John Wynne must have given much thought to the future of his country. So did Sir Robert Peel. Peel had been Chief Secretary for Ireland from 1812 to 1818 and was Prime Minister for the second time from 1841 to 1846 during part of the famine years. In 1849 he wrote to Wynne in the following terms:

" Drayton Manor, April 13, 1849.
My Dear Sir,
There is no one whose concurrence in any general views as to the condition of Ireland which I had expressed could give me greater confidence in their soundness than yours.

66

I well know that there is no one more deeply interested in the welfare of Ireland or a better judge of the means of promoting it.

I believe that a great calamity offers us a great opportunity - not for sudden change for the better - but for laying gradually the foundation of a better order of things.

Since I came here I have been reading the evidence taken by the Lords and Commons Committees on the Poor Laws.

That evidence, as might be expected, has reference rather to the condition of landed property in Ireland and the social state and prospects of the country than to the particular matters for the investigation of which they were appointed.

I know not how anyone can resist the conclusion that after spending nine millions for the relief of the destitute we have done little more than save a given number of persons from starvation, that we have not effected this unquestionable good without the alloy of much evil, without disturbing the natural demand for labour and diminishing the inducements to self reliance and industry.

I fear very little has been done to prevent the recurrence of the very same evils from which we have been suffering for the last four years. Two or three abundant potato crops will soon ensure the filling up of the diminished ranks of the destitute, we shall have the same blind confidence and in a very short time the same cause for repentance that we had not profited by the warning which should have stimulated us to break through the vicious circle of the past.

I have heard many arguments directed against positions which I have never maintained - none which have weakened my conviction that there is an urgent necessity for some extraordinary intervention especially in respect to the extrication of landed property in Ireland from the impediments to its free transfer.

Believe me, my dear sir,
Most faithfully yours,
Robert Peel".

What Peel had in mind was the urgent necessity for the redistribution of Irish land. Elsewhere he had described the system of land holding in Ireland as 'a monstrous evil'. The impediments to such a redistribution were many. One of the foremost was lack of capital on the part of would-be buyers. This also inhibited tenants from farming with any degree of success which in turn increased the difficulty of paying the rent. And rents were high because of the competition for tenancies. In such circum-

Drayton Manor April 13.
1849

My dear Sir

There is no urgent necessity for extraordinary intervention concurrence in ... especially in respect views at ... the cultivation of lands ... property & Ireland ... give me ... their ... for the impediments to its free ...

Believe me ... most faithfully yours
Robert Peel

stances any advance in the science of agriculture was almost impossible. Peel's phrase 'the extrication of landed property from the impediments to its free transfer' referred also to the plight of landlords. They too for the most part lacked capital, a situation made worse by the inevitable fall in their rents as a result of the famine. Indeed in 1849 an Encumbered Estates Act was passed which facilitated the sale of mortgaged land through a special court. Peel fell from power before his Irish policy could be developed, and he left the legacy of the land question to his principal disciple Gladstone who began the process by which the ownership of land was transferred from landlord to tenant through the Land Commission.

It was mentioned in the previous chapter that the young Lord Palmerston had visited Owen Wynne V at Hazelwood in 1808. In the middle of the century Palmerston, by then Foreign Secretary for the third time, was a frequent visitor to the county while his home Classiebawn was being planned and the harbour at Mullaghmore constructed. Palmerston's reputation was stained by reports of the deplorable condition of his tenants on their arrival as emigrants at St. John, New Brunswick, and at Quebec, which provoked a protest from the Governor–General of Canada. But O'Rorke pictures him as a benevolent landlord and a benefactor of those tenants who remained at home, through the draining of bog, the planting of bent to prevent further erosion from the sea, and the building of schools. He did not leave these matters to his agent. In a letter from Cliffony to John Wynne dated the 26th September, 1844, Palmerston wrote:

" *I have been very busy in squaring the holdings or townlands and thus giving each tenant a separate holding. I trust that this arrangement will put an end to the standing quarrel between McGowan and Harrison, as well as to many other feuds which have long disturbed the domestic peace of this district"*.

Lady Palmerston, who had been asked by Wynne for a subscription to his Protestant Orphans' Charity, wrote as part of her reply:

" *I assure you that I always take a great interest in Sligo and am very happy to hear of any improvements there. It would indeed be of great benefit if we could have the railway you mention and I hope from your account that this may come to pass. The next thing I wish for is that we could have some change in our horrid inn at Sligo. It is such a nasty dirty place and this with such a good situation that ought I think to produce a nice tidy inn"*.

At the time there were numerous inns in Sligo. The one that Lady Palmerston referred to was probably the Nelson, which occupied the

Dear Mr Wynne
Many thanks
for your letter I
am very glad to hear
our Bishops have
had so large a benefit
from our small Sub...
and I have written
to Mrs Kincaid to beg
her will pay you
the amount as before

to many other funds
which have long ...
the domestic peace of
this district.
Many thanks for
what you say about
Erasmuway and I will
request Mr Kincaid to
communicate with you
on the subject
Yrs sincerely
Palmerston

John Wynne

Cliffony 26 Sept 1845

Dear Wynne
I am very sorry
to find that we shall
not have the pleasure
of finding you at
Hazlewood on Tuesday,
and unfortunately we
are so tied up as to time
that we cannot put off
our visit till your
return from Gorbal...

produce a ...
... but W S ...
long leases, and the
there were many
difficulties in the ...
of any improvement
...... are done ...
Wynne
Yrs very sincerely
E Palmerston
Brocket Hall.
Welwyn
... 12th
How beautiful your ...
look in this fine hot weather

70

building which is now the Imperial Hotel. No doubt it was the best available. John Wynne lived long enough to see the extension of the Midland Great Western Railway from Longford to Sligo in 1862. It was left to his son, Owen VI, to be one of the promoters and one of the first directors of the Sligo, Leitrim and Northern Counties Railway which was completed in 1882. The Act of Parliament which gave authority for this railway to be built listed the following names as the principal promoters:

ARTHUR LOFTUS TOTTENHAM, GLENFARNE HALL, A GUARANTOR FOR
£5,000 AND FIRST CHAIRMAN.
VISCOUNT COLE.
OWEN WYNNE, A GUARANTOR FOR £3,000 AND ONE OF THE
INITIAL FIVE DIRECTORS.
LORD MASSEY, A GUARANTOR FOR £5,000 AND ONE
OF THE ORIGINAL DIRECTORS.
THOMAS MORRIS HAMILTON JONES.
FRANCIS LA TOUCHE, A GUARANTOR FOR £1,000 AND DEPUTY CHAIRMAN.
THE EARL OF ENNISKILLEN, A GUARANTOR FOR £1,000.
R.E. DAVIES OF LURGANBOY.
SIR ROBERT GORE–BOOTH OF LISSADELL.
HENRY WILLIAM GORE–BOOTH OF LISSADELL.

In 1856 John Wynne re–entered politics and was elected for the Borough by a majority of 31 votes in a total poll of 265; the poll shows the restricted nature of the franchise even after the Reform Act. His opponent was the John Patrick Somers who had defeated John Martin in 1837. As a bon viveur and a lover of the stage and the turf, Somers appears to have been a much more colourful personality than Wynne. In 1846 he had fought a duel at Camphill, Collooney, supposedly the last duel fought in Ireland. In 1857 when Wynne and Somers contested the seat again, Somers was declared elected by one vote. Wynne petitioned to unseat his opponent. The evidence given before the committee of Parliament which considered the petition describes how (before the introduction in 1872 of the secret ballot) a voter called out the name of his candidate in the Courthouse. On this occasion the Courthouse was crowded with non-voters crying out "Somers, Somers, Somers". The poll clerk rejected some voters for failing to give their second forename when declaring their identity, although he knew each of them personally. A witness named Martin Feenarty said that a week before the poll a Somers mob had broken into several houses causing Feenarty and his friends to take refuge in the Courthouse for seven days and nights. When the unfortunate Feenarty came to vote the poll clerk called out: "Take him away, he is very drunk". The committee decided that Somers should be unseated and Wynne declared elected after three Somers votes were transferred to Wynne and a further three votes of voters who were rejected by the poll clerk were awarded to Wynne.

Bribery and violence reached their peak in the election of 1868 when the candidates were John Woulfe Flanagan, Liberal, and Laurence Knox, the proprietor of the Irish Times, Conservative. After the election a commission, which sat in Sligo, unseated Knox, the successful candidate. Its report reviewed the extent of corruption in this and previous elections and criticised the Bishop of Elphin, Dr. Gillooly, for exercising undue influence by threatening spiritual pains and penalties against those who did not vote for Flanagan. Parliament had had enough. In 1870 the Borough constituency was abolished by a Disfranchisement Act.

Wynne had been re–elected in 1859, but advancing ill–health caused him to resign a year later. He had served his community well. He was chairman of the Board of Guardians, the body responsible for the relief of poverty, between 1847 and 1852. He helped to found the Sligo mental hospital. He continued his father's work in agriculture and afforestation; he was responsible for planting the silver firs on the Hazelwood demesne, while at Glencar he planted black Austrian pine, Scotch fir, oak, elm and larch.

John Wynne died in 1865 at the age of 64. A memorial tablet in Calry church concludes with the words:

> *"The tenants of the Estates, who for forty years enjoyed the benefit of his unceasing labours to promote their domestic prosperity; being desirous of perpetuating their deep sense of his worth and, in gratitude to The Giver of All Good, have raised this tablet in his memory"*.

John Wynne, his wife Lady Anne, and his daughter Sarah were all talented amateur artists. They drew well and painted charming landscapes of scenes around Hazelwood and in Italy. A number of albums containing their drawings and paintings survive, and these were the subject of an exhibition at the Sligo Art Gallery in 1990. John Wynne was also a pioneer botanist. He was not merely a lover of wild flowers, but a close and scientific observer of the alpine flora of Benbulben and the adjoining limestone mountains. He was the first to discover on these mountains a number of rare plants.

CHAPTER TWELVE

A Valuation of the Property

In the 1830's and 1840's Owen Wynne V and his son John Arthur Wynne caused to be made numerous surveys of the extent and value of the estate. As this period represents the high water mark of the family's fortunes, it is appropriate to extract from the documents figures which provide a picture of the economic background to the history of the family at that time.

The acreage of the estate, not including property in the town of Sligo, was as follows:–

PARISH OF DRUMCLIFF	5,843
PARISH OF CALRY	3,756
DETACHED TOWNLANDS	1,008
LAND IN WYNNE'S OWN HANDS	1,956
CO. LEITRIM	15,513
	28,076 ACRES

Within the town of Sligo the following were owned by the family:-

Abbey Quarter, Bridge Street, Church Lane, Forthill, Holborn Street, John's Lane, High Street, The Lungy, Market Street, Quay Street, Radcliffe Street and Stephen Street, together with the adjacent townlands of Ballinode, Belvoir and Carns.

In 1833 William Dix, Owen Wynne's solicitor in Dublin, compiled a valuation of the Wynne property, real and personal. The following are particulars:-

PERSONAL PROPERTY: TOTAL £44,000
WOODS (ROCKWOOD, LURGANBOY, HAZELWOOD, DOONEE *[BOUGHT FOR £800 20 YEARS EARLIER]*, BELVOIR].
LIVE AND DEAD STOCK, PLATE, FURNITURE, WINE, PICTURES, BOOKS, BOATS, ETC. £10,000 PLUS DEBT OF £7,000 OWED BY RICHARD WYNNE.

LAND: TOTAL	£335,250
ESTATE OF SLIGO	175,000
LEITRIM ESTATE, COMPRISING 800	
LEASES AT LOW RENTS	20,750
BISHOPS' LEASES	43,000
HAZELWOOD DEMESNE, 540 ACRES	
WITH BUILDINGS WORTH £20,000	50,000
BELVOIR ESTATE, 154 ACRES	6,000
MARKETS IN SLIGO	30,000
FEE FARM LEASES IN DUBLIN	
(rents £80)	1,600
DEERPARK 170 ACRES	5,000
THREE ISLANDS	300
SUNDRY PROFITS ON LEASES	1,500
LAND ON WHICH ROCKWOOD AND	
LURGANBOY WOODS STAND,	
SUPPOSING THEM TO BE CUT	2,600
	£335,250

Thus on Dix's valuation the total for real and personal property was £379,750.

Dix calculated the annual income as follows:-

RENTS

SLIGO ESTATE	£ 7,135
LURGANBOY ESTATE	800
ARDAGH BISHOP'S LEASE	1,450
KILMORE BISHOP'S LEASE	2,008
PROFIT RENTS	135
ANNUAL PROFITS OF MARKETS	1,500
DEMESNE AND PRODUCE OF THINNING	
WOODS	500
PRODUCE OF WOOL, CATTLE, ETC. SOLD	
OFF FARM	500
BELVOIR AND THE DEERPARK IN MR.	
WYNNE'S OWN HANDS	350
TOTAL	£14,458

To these figures Dix added the following note'*The above is a low computation of the annual value of lands held by Mr. Wynne in his own hands. If set (i.e. let) to tenants it would produce much more by the year. Some of the leases are for old lives which are frequently falling in and*

74

thereby considerably improving the value of the property. A great portion of the town of Sligo is built on Mr. Wynne's estate.'

The figures in Dix's valuation are gross figures and they do not reflect the true position. They omit two important factors, namely the extent to which the estate was mortgaged, and the large amounts by which the payment of rent was in arrears.

First, then, mortgages. The fact that the estate was heavily mortgaged need cause no surprise. Until the development, particularly in the second half of the 19th century, of the joint stock company with shareholders and limited liability, wealth lay almost exclusively in land. If a landowner needed to make a large capital outlay, for example to build or rebuild his house, or to pay for an expensive parliamentary election, he could do so only by mortgaging an appropriate portion of his land. For the mortgagee (the lender) the procedure represented a method of investing his money so as to draw a regular income. In effect he became the equivalent of a debenture holder in a modern limited liability company.

A list of mortgages relating to the Wynne estate sets out the mortgages between 1754 and 1833. The sums lent vary between a few hundred pounds to as much as £13,000. The lenders are sometimes members of the family or relations, such as the Earl of Enniskillen, but for the most part are substantial townspeople whose names are familiar from local histories. From time to time mortgages were redeemed, but the total owed by the Wynne family in 1833 was £102,370.

The larger mortgages were made necessary by marriage. Each of the two families concerned contributed to the marriage settlement. On the Wynne side the contribution consisted of land which was to be mortgaged; on the bride's side it consisted of a capital sum, which could be described as a dowry. One cannot fail to notice in the settlements the extent of the Wynne family's debts. We are concerned here with three such settlements, those relating to the marriages of Owen Wynne IV, Owen Wynne V and John Arthur Wynne.

In 1754 Owen Wynne IV married Anne Maxwell. At the time Owen's father was still alive. Anne's father contributed £10,000, £8,000 of which was for the elder Wynne (Owen III) and £2,000 for his son. The two Wynnes conveyed to trustees land sufficient to pay an annuity of £1,000 p.a. to Anne during her widowhood. The trustees were to raise a further £3,000 by way of sale or mortgage of other Wynne lands for the discharge of Owen III's debts and those incumbrances which were left unsatisfied after the payment to him of the £8,000 referred to above. In addition the trustees raised a further £10,000 on Wynne lands for the benefit of the younger children of the marriage.

The bridegroom, who two years after his marriage became Owen Wynne IV, had under the settlement the power to appoint, that is to distribute at his discretion the £10,000 between his younger children. He had six sons and three daughters. To his youngest daughter Catherine, he appointed part of the sum on her marriage to the Rev. Euseby Cleaver. The rest he divided in his will amongst the daughters who had married. They received roughly equal shares, except for his daughter Judith who, "because she had married without his privity, consent or approbation and to disoblige him" received only five shillings. Judith had married Patrick Cullen. One might have thought that Owen Wynne's unforgiving attitude towards this daughter was caused by the fact that Patrick was a member of that prominent family of Cullen who had distinguished themselves on the Catholic side in the rising of 1641, the Cromwellian conquest and the Williamite war, but in fact he was a member of a Protestant family from Skreeny, County Leitrim. It is unlikely that we shall ever know all the reasons for Owen Wynne's disapproval of Patrick Cullen. But in 1780 at about the time of Judith Wynne's marriage, Cullen lent on mortgage to Owen Wynne and his son (later Owen V) the substantial sum of £7,300. The property mortgaged by the Wynnes was extensive and included not only a number of townlands but also the following built up areas in the town of Sligo, viz Abbey Quarter, Bridge Street, Church Lane, Ratcliffe Street (now Grattan Street), John's Lane, Holbourne Street and Stephen Street. The agreement was a very onerous one as far as the Wynnes were concerned for under it Cullen, so long as the money lent was not repaid, became entitled not only to interest but also to the rents of the mortgaged property. On top of all this he became entitled to the tolls and customs of the fairs and markets. It is possible that Cullen drove a hard bargain when the Wynnes were in serious need of liquid capital and that Owen IV was not willing to forgive him.

A year after Owen IV's death in 1799, his eldest son, Owen V, married Lady Sarah Elizabeth Cole. Sarah brought into the marriage settlement £10,500 to which she was entitled under the will of her grandmother. £8,750 of this was to be used in the discharge of the Wynnes' debts and mortgages. The balance, together with £12,000 which the trustees had power to raise by sale or mortgage of Wynne lands, was to be used to pay Sarah £300 p.a. during her widowhood, together with portions for the younger children. The trustees raised part of the £12,000 by selling the lands in County Cavan, which had been bought from the Duke of Wharton, together with some of the Dublin property. A further

£4,000 was raised by the sale of land when Owen V's daughter Anne married the Earl of Carrick.

Since the family's statement of title stops at 1823 we do not have particulars of the marriage settlement of 1838 when John Arthur Wynne married Lady Anne Butler. The Wynne papers contain 'a list of lands in Mr. John Wynne's marriage settlement'' but this does not give any figures, so that a rough calculation must suffice. We have seen above that the mortgage debt in 1833 was just over £100,000. On this sum interest at 5 per cent would be £5,000 p.a. We will see below that John Arthur was paying £7,000 by way of such interest. The increase from £5,000 to £7,000 represents a further £40,000 raised by mortgage.

It can now be seen that Dix's valuation of 1833, concerned as it is only with gross figures, does not reflect the net value of the estate. As to income the true picture is provided by an updated and informal calculation in the handwriting of John Arthur Wynne. This note is as follows:-

GROSS

Rental	£14,240
Hazelwood	1,000
Dividends	130
Grazing	120
Tolls	660
Town Hall	50
	£16,200

NETT

Rents	1,606
Rentcharge	331
Interest	7,000
Annuities	320
Insurance	950
County cess	320
Management	950
Income Tax	250
Poor rates	335
Costs	250
Discounts	120
Allowances	150
Miscellaneous	400
	£12,982

Balance of income over expenditure : £3,218

Some of the above figures require comment. In the Gross column the income from tolls represents the amount received after payment of the expenses of the market and the payment of the wages of those employed there. In the Nett column the figure for rents includes the rents payable for the bishops' leases and the rent of land leased by the Wynnes for such purposes as commercial forestry. Interest relates to the interest on mortgages. County cess is the sum payable as rates to the Grand Jury. The poor rates were payable to the Poor Law Guardians. Management represents the expenses, including wages, of the demesne and other lands kept in the Wynnes' own hands, but excluding domestic servants.

Finally, a list of labourers exists for the years 1833 and 1836. The term 'labourers' probably included not only agriculture labourers, but also stonemasons and carpenters. The numbers employed are:-

      1833   71
      1836   63

The names in the two lists are for the most part the same. Daily rates of pay varied from 7 pence to one shilling and three pence. The total weekly bill in 1833 was £15–12–0 and in 1836 £13–12–6.

CHAPTER THIRTEEN

Wynne Power Dismantled

Background

The 19th century witnessed the end of the power and influence of the Anglo-Irish ascendancy. The first step in this process was taken by the Act of Union in 1800. It was intended that this measure should be followed immediately by Catholic emancipation which would have enabled Catholics to become members of Parliament and to hold any public office. Unfortunately, owing to the opposition of Peel and George III, emancipation was not conceded until 1829. This delay resulted in O'Connell's campaign for emancipation followed by his campaign for repeal of the Act of Union. Both movements attracted massive public support. In consequence Catholicism and nationalism became linked together in the public mind. Inevitably Protestantism would lose ground and then become of minor importance when the nationalist aspirations of the country were achieved.

In 1869 the Church of Ireland was disestablished by an Act of the Westminister Parliament. The Church had been a prop of the ascendancy. Now Catholic tenants no longer had to pay tithes to a church which was not their own. While no fair minded person could regret this step, yet from then on the Church of Ireland inevitably declined as a factor in the life of the nation.

Above all the Land Acts at the turn of the new century transferred the ownership of land from Protestant landlord to Catholic tenant. It was under these Acts, as we shall see in the following chapter, that the larger part of the Wynne estate was sold.

Parliamentary and Local Government

The Reform Act of 1832 put an end to 'rotten' or 'pocket' boroughs where the choice of the member of Parliament was effectively by nomination not by election. By that Act the direct power of the Wynne family to appoint the member for the Borough of Sligo was removed. In boroughs and counties the franchise was conferred on householders of a dwelling house of at least £10 annual value. It was as a result of this change that John Martin was able to defeat John Arthur Wynne in the election of 1837. In fact John Arthur Wynne's other contests, which we have already looked at and which were hardly models of parliamentary democracy, were made necessary by the Reform Act. The extension of the franchise in stages throughout the century substantially increased the Catholic vote.

Before reform the local authority for the Borough of Sligo consisted of two bodies, the Corporation and the Town and Harbour Commissioners. The Corporation, consisting of the provost (mayor), freemen and burgesses, was nothing but a self-perpetuating oligarchy under the control of the Wynnes. The Town and Harbour Commissioners, whose powers were not restricted to the port, were set up in 1803. They were elected by £20 freeholders. The provost and burgesses, together with the members of Parliament for the Borough and County, were ex–officio members. The elected members numbered twenty four and were elected for life. A majority of this body was controlled by the Wynnes. Some measure of reform came with the Municipal Corporations (Ireland) Act, 1840, by which local councils became elective on the same franchise as that for parliamentary elections, but the Town and Harbour Commissioners were left untouched.

The most important local government body in the County was the Grand Jury. Its powers extended over the construction of roads and bridges, the appointment of the administrative staff of the County and the provision and upkeep of infirmaries and asylums. It was the equivalent of the then County Quarter Sessions in England. This body was wholly undemocratic; it was appointed each year from among members of the larger landowning families by the High Sheriff for the time being, who was himself always a Protestant landlord. Its revenue was derived from a tax on land called the county cess. Whereas the Borough Council could raise a rate of only threepence in the pound, the Grand Jury had power to raise an limited rate in both County and Borough. Much criticism was levelled at it for its award of contracts on the basis of jobbery, patronage and nepotism. One or more members of the Wynne family always appeared amongst its numbers. By a private Act, the Sligo Borough Improvement Act of 1869, the Grand Jury lost its power to levy cess within the Borough, so that the corporation became responsible for all services within the town. The latter body made a much needed start on providing a clean water supply and on lighting and paving the streets. By the same Act the Town and Harbour Commissioners were dissolved; their place was taken by new Harbour Commissioners, no longer elected for life, whose powers were restricted to the harbour only. Finally, by the Local Government Act of 1898 Grand Juries were abolished, their place being taken by elected County Councils. By slow stages democracy, albeit with some way to go, had replaced an oligarchy largely dominated by the Wynnes.

Tolls and Customs

We have already seen that with the purchase of the Strafford -Radcliffe land in 1722 the Wynne family had acquired the right to hold a market in Sligo and to levy tolls on goods sold in the market. In 1834 a select committee of Parliament enquired into the fairs and markets of Ireland. Witnesses who gave evidence relating to Sligo described the market there as a large building in the centre of a large yard. Corn and other produce was brought there from seven or eight counties. At Wynne expense an inspector was provided, together with assistants to unload, weigh and load the goods. The duty of the inspector was to detect fraud; for example a sack could contain bad grain in the centre and good grain at both ends. The evidence before the committee showed that sellers preferred to have their produce weighed on the market scales rather than on the scales of private merchants, for the latter's scales were often adjusted in favour of the buyer. The evidence also showed the profits accruing to the Wynne family. The average amount of tolls received during the previous five years was £1,555 per annum, while the expenses amounted to an average of £998 per annum, leaving an annual net profit of £557.

The new Borough Council elected under the Municipal Corporations Act of 1840 was evidently not happy about the market and its tolls, for at its first meeting it appointed a committee to examine whether tolls and customs were properly payable and, if so, to whom. The committee was no doubt satisfied as to the legality of the Wynne claim, but as we shall see the matter was not to be allowed to rest there.

The Wynnes had another source of profit from the trade of the town. By the Irish Butter Act of 1812 the price of butter was regulated by law, and to fix the price of a consignment of butter brought into a market the office of Weighmaster and Taster of Butter was established. In Sligo the position was held first by Owen Wynne V and after him by his son John Arthur Wynne. Both carried out the duties of the office by appointing a a paid deputy to grade the butter into different categories according to quality, but the Wynnes kept the fees payable under the Act for this service. On John Arthur Wynne's death in 1865 the Corporation elected its mayor, James Tighe, to the office of Weighmaster and Taster. John's son, Owen VI, resorted to law to contest this appointment, but in the litigation Tighe was not surprisingly successful.

Finally, the Sligo Borough Improvement Act, 1869, gave the Corporation the power to establish fairs, markets and slaughterhouses within the Borough and to purchase from Owen Wynne VI his rights relating to fairs and markets together with the buildings relating to them. Eventually terms were agreed. Wynne was paid £6,500 and the right which his family had owned since 1722 became extinct.

My Dear Mr Wynne,
I am going to Sligo the first thing tomorrow morning and from thence to Manorhamilton. I propose to return from there in the afternoon and if this will not be taking you by storm, it will give me much pleasure to go to you on my return from Manorhamilton.

Will you kindly send a reply to the Gate House on the Manorhamilton Road, I will call and ask if I am admitted,

*Believe me,
Yours Very Sincerely, Leitrim.*

LETTER FROM LORD LEITRIM, LOUGH RYNN, FEB. 5th 1878

CHAPTER FOURTEEN

Owen Wynne VI
1843 - 1910

OWEN WYNNE VI

Owen Wynne VI succeeded to the family estates in 1865 at the age of twenty three. In his youth he had served as a lieutenant in the 61st Foot Regiment and, as one would expect, he was High Sheriff of County Sligo in 1875 and of County Leitrim in 1881. At the age of 27 he married Stella Fanny, the younger daughter of Sir Robert Gore-Booth of Lissadell, the fourth baronet.

The second half of the 19th century saw the development of what is recognisably modern Ireland. Post-famine Ireland was at first exhausted and dispirited, but events were moving towards a resolution of the landlord–tenant conflict. As early as 1850 a Tenant Right Association had demanded the 'three F's', namely fair rent, fixity of tenure and freedom for the tenant to sell his leasehold interest. A new impetus was given by the foundation in 1858 in Dublin and New York of the Irish Republican Brotherhood (Fenians). In the face of falling prices and crop failures, Michael Davitt founded the Land League. Thus began the 'land war' of 1879 to 1882, perhaps generally remembered for the invention of the word 'boycott,' from Lord Erne's agent in Mayo.

STELLA FANNY WYNNE
Wife of Owen(née Gore-Booth),who was accidently killed, 27th Feb 1887

The Land League organised mass meetings of tenants throughout Ireland. On the 22nd August, 1880, such a meeting was held at Manor-hamilton at which 7,000 people and six bands were present. In the course of his speech to the crowd, the chairman, James Cullen said:-

"Landlordism surely requires reform, though there are certainly some landlords who are creditably different from the majority. Mr. Wynne, and some others like him, are a credit to the name of landlord. The idle few, not at home, but abroad or in England, leave their lands to the tender mercies of a horde of agents and bailiffs".

The Land League was followed by the National League, after the former had been outlawed. Although Land Courts had been set up by the Gladstone administration in 1881 to fix fair rents, and although rents had been reduced by an average of 10 per cent, tenants needed more protection. The National League in 1886 set in motion the Plan of Campaign. Tenants were to combine. Where a landlord refused to lower the rents voluntarily, the tenants offered reduced rents. If this offer was not accepted the tenants were to pay no rent at all, but instead paid an equivalent amount into a fund to be used for the support of those who were evicted. In County Leitrim the plan was first put into action in December, 1886, on Owen Wynne's estate, for the agent, George Hewson, refused a proposed reduction of 25 per cent. Proinnsios O Duigneain, from whose 'North Leitrim : The Land War and the Fall of Parnell' (1988) this information is taken, makes the following comment:

> "The decision of the League to choose the Wynne estate for the plan may have been influenced by the fact that the landlord was not considered harsh in his dealing with tenants and, therefore, the achievement of a favourable settlement within a short time was a real possibility. On the other hand local leaders may have desired a confrontation with George Hewson, which would give them the opportunity of undermining his reputation as one of the most feared agents in the country".

This comment would appear to be well–founded. In a book entitled 'The North-West of Ireland" published in 1862, the author, Henry Coulter, paints a grim picture of the poverty and wretched living conditions of the inhabitants of that part of the country. By contrast, in a chapter on Co. Leitrim, he writes as follows:

> "A few miles from the town of Manorhamilton there is a large tract of land belonging to the Right Hon. John Wynne. The population is numerous and they are, comparatively speaking, in a comfortable condition. Mr. Wynne's land is let at a low rent - from 14s to 15s per acre for land of fair quality. He is a most liberal and indulgent landlord, and is greatly respected and loved by those who hold under him. I entered into conversation with an intelligent man, holding about fourteen acres, in addition to which he has four acres of bog, which he reclaimed, and had sown with oats last year. I saw some of the oats grown on the bog and the quality of the grain was excellent, whilst the produce was abundant. He had sown potatoes previously, manured with lime and farm–yard manure, and he prepared the soil for oats by mixing blue clay and sand, which he obtained on his farm, with the peaty soil. In the course of time these four acres of bog will be converted into good arable land. At present he pays no rent for this, and Mr. Wynne has promised him that as long as he holds the farm of fourteen acres, he shall have the reclaimed land rent free. This man has a good substantial dwelling–house and an excellent cow–house and dairy. He has six or seven milch cows, and as many more one and two–year old heifers, all of which were comfortably housed and well provided with fodder. There are a good many other

tenants of Mr. Wynne equally well off; but on the neighbouring estates it would be difficult to find similar instances of prosperity amongst the small holders, and they are nearly all of that class in this part of the country".

The landlord referred to in this passage was of course Owen Wynne's father, who lived for three years after the publication of Coulter's book, but there is no reason to think that there was any change in policy when Owen VI inherited his father's property.

The land war could have caused little surprise to a landlord such as Wynne. One may conjecture that he had disapproved of the activities of his neighbour, Lord Leitrim of Lough Rynn, Dromad. Lord Leitrim owned large estates in Leitrim, Donegal and Galway over which he exercised a personal tyranny. He refused to recognise Ulster tenant right, which applied to Donegal, and ranted against it in the House of Commons, of which as an Irish peer, he was a member. He was disliked by his fellow landlords as much as by his tenants. On the 5th February, 1878, he wrote to Owen Wynne to say that he proposed to visit Wynne on the following day, adding "if this will not be taking you by storm". He requested Wynne to leave a reply at his gate-house where, Lord Leitrim said, he would "call and ask if I am admitted". Two months later when the Earl was driving in a side-car through the Fanad peninsula in Donegal he was ambushed near Kindrum by three men who had rowed across the upper waters of Mulroy Bay. Although aged 72, he put up a fight but was felled and killed by a blow from the butt of a gun. His clerk and driver were also murdered. A side-car containing police which it was intended should accompany him was far behind, for a smith had intentionally lamed the horse. A monument later erected near the scene of these events commemorates not the victims but the murderers who 'by their heroic action put an end to the tyranny of the landlords'. These words are a translation from the Gaelic inscription. But the claim was premature, for at that time the land war was still to come.

The reduction of rents and the prevailing agricultural depression, together with a background of violence and disorder, persuaded many landlords that the Land League ideal of a peasant ownership of the land was the only solution. Land transfer had already begun under *Ashbourne's Act* of 1885 and was completed under *Wyndham's Act* of 1903. Each side stood to gain. The landlord was paid a capital sum on a calculation of so many years' purchase (up to 28 years) on the rents fixed by the Land Courts, while the tenant was to repay the purchase price

86

A PHAETON OUTSIDE HAZELWOOD. *In the driving seat is Sarah, sister to Owen VI. Behind Sarah from LtoR are Owen's three daughters, Evelyn (later Mrs Henry George L'Estrange), Muriel and Dorothy. In the centre is Henderson, the butler, while Martin, the coachman, holds the horse's head*

SHOOTING PARTY AT HAZELWOOD IN THE 1890'S.
Owen Wynne VI with his sisters Sarah and Grace are on the left. The rest are guests, with the gamekeeper with his gun on his shoulder.

advanced by the government over a period of 68 years at a low rate of interest. Under these provisions Owen Wynne sold his estates, other than the Hazelwood demesne, to the Land Commission for the price of £79,000. This represents about four million pounds at the present day. Under *Wyndham's Act* landlordism as it had previously been known in Ireland came to an end.

On Sunday, the 27th February, 1887, Mrs. Wynne suffered a serious accident which caused her death. She had been to Calry church in the morning and in the afternoon set out with a companion, Miss McClintock, for Capt. Peel's house at Newtownmanor, from where they intended to go to the afternoon church service. She drove a phaeton, a light four–wheeled vehicle drawn by one horse. The horse was young, having only lately been broken to harness, and the shafts of the phaeton were too short, so that the front of the vehicle tended to rub against the hindquarters of the horse. Colga and Fermoyle were safely passed but as they approached Fivemilebourne the horse bolted. Mrs. Wynne handed the whip to her companion, took a firm grip of the reins and tried to pull up the horse. As they went downhill following a slight crest in the road the front wheels came off and the horse rushed wildly on with the front part of the phaeton scraping along the ground. The collapse of the front wheels caused the two ladies to be thrown out. Miss McClintock landed on the grass verge and was uninjured, but Mrs. Wynne was thrown against a boulder which served as a gatepost. The phaeton came to rest lying on its side, shattered and broken; the horse was caught and ridden back at a gallop to Sligo for medical help. Mrs. Wynne was carried into the house of Michael Hargadon. The doctor when he arrived found she had suffered a fractured skull. She was nursed at the Hargadons' house, but died two days later.

Of this melancholy event O'Rorke, in rather flowery language, writes as follows:

"It is agreed on all sides that the ladies of the Hazelwood family have been conspicuous for the faithful and exemplary discharge of the duties incumbent on the high social station which they held in the neighbourhood. Though Lady Sarah, the wife of Mr. Owen Wynne, died as far back as 1833, the memory of her almsgiving and other charities is still fresh all round the parish of Calry; Lady Anne Wynne was equally devoted to the poor and miserable; and it was the Good Samaritan virtues, and the exquisitely womanly sensibilities and sympathies, in regard to the suffering classes, of the late Mrs. Wynne -

*much more than any other circumstances connected with her beauti-
ful life, or singularly sad death – which, on the day of her decease
sent a thrill of sorrow through every household, high and low, in the
county, and on the day of her funeral attracted after her honoured
remains such crowds of rich and poor, Protestants and Catholics, as,
up to that time, were unparalleled in the county of Sligo for numbers
and the feelings that swayed them, and are little likely to be paral-
leled there again in these respects, for a long time to come".*

Since the Wynnes of Hazelwood were just about to come to their end,
it is of interest to consider what the house and its demesne were like
before the sunset finally faded. O'Rorke, who published his History in
1889, wrote a contemporary account:-

*"Though the residence may not be equal in massiveness to some
more modern mansions, it is still a very stately and graceful struc-
ture. It is built of cut and polished limestone, in the Italian style, with
a bold four-storey front facade, and two lateral curving wings, after
the manner of a peristyle. The hall door is reached by a noble flight
of stone steps landing onto a spacious platform which commands a
good view of the Leitrim and North Sligo mountains. A secondary
front, rising from a fine terrace, looks to the south; and the area,
running form the terrace to the lake, is divided between an open lawn
and shady groves, in which are provided charming retreats for saun-
terers, including a cane house, a rock house, a shell house (which
had the inside walls covered with sea shells), and a curious chair of
state constructed of materials rarely found in these latitudes, the
bones of the whale".*

O'Rorke continued by saying that the cape running into Lough Gill, on
which the mansion stood, was covered with trees and shrubs, in particular
arbutus.

In 1912 the Irish Farming World published an article entitled 'Hazelwood, Sligo, and its Management'. At that time Owen VI had been dead
for two years and in another nine years the farm stock and machinery
were to be sold. But from the article one may obtain a picture of the
Hazelwood demesne as it was at the time of the last Owen Wynne. The
details may be summarized as follows. The estate consisted of 900 acres
of arable land, of which 80 were under tillage, 130 in meadow, and the
balance of 690 acres under grazing. A further 600 acres were under
forestry, which provided coverts particularly for shooting woodcock.
There were seven miles of roads which were maintained by a stone

crusher driven by a traction engine, and a considerable amount of labour was saved by 'a neat French railway'. (What, one wonders, was that?). Successional plantings had been made of larch, spruce and scotch and silver fir for commercial purposes. In the arboretum were some of the finest ornamental conifers in the country. Around the house there were gardens and pleasure grounds, and the home farm. A hundred head of cattle were bred annually, chiefly Aberdeen Angus crosses. The bull had been bred in Lord Rothchild's herd at Tring. There were twenty to twenty-five dairy cows and seventy to eighty ewes. An oil engine pumped water to the house, and a steam engine drove the threshing machinery and the sawmill. There was stabling for thirty horses. £1,500 was expended annually on labour, which included two carpenters, two blacksmiths and two masons. The workmen, who were succeeded by their sons and their sons' sons, were comfortably housed and their cottages had an air of comfort and happiness.

Hazelwood was the venue for many sporting events. Yacht racing on Lough Gill took place throughout the 19th century. The scene could be an animated one; one account dating from 1823 described how a crowd of 12,000 to 15,000 persons watched a race from the slopes of Belvoir while, in addition to the competing yachts, between thirty and forty sailing boats and rowing boats carried spectators on the lake. The length of the course was eighteen miles which entailed sailing twice round the lake. From 1880 to 1942 race meetings were held on the race–course on the Hazelwood demesne. A polo club was founded in 1878, the home matches being played at Hazelwood. The principal players were Major C.K. O'Hara of Annaghmore, a notable player, Capt. W. Campbell, Major Eccles, Capt. Maxwell, C.A. L'Estrange, A. Lyons and Henry Tottenham. According to the *Sligo Champion* a game at Hazelwood was an event to be watched by the entire town. Sligo polo ponies were much in demand and many were exported to England and America.

Owen Wynne VI died in 1910 aged 67. One cannot escape the feeling that he was a saddened man. His wife had been tragically killed twenty-three years earlier. The great estates of 15,000 acres in Leitrim and 14,000 acres in Sligo had for the most part been sold. Since he had no male heir, with his death the line of the Wynnes of Hazelwood came to an end.

CHAPTER FIFTEEN

Hazelwood after the Wynnes

Owen Wynne VI left four daughters. His eldest daughter and heiress, Muriel, married in 1892 Philip Dudley Perceval, the youngest son of Alexander Perceval of Temple House, Co. Sligo. In 1901 his second daughter Evelyn Mary, married Henry George L'Estrange, the youngest son of Christopher Carleton L'Estrange of Market Hill, Co. Fermanagh and Kevinsfort, Sligo. His two other daughters remained unmarried.

From 1910 to 1923 Mr. and Mrs. Perceval lived at Hazelwood. A year before they left Mrs. Perceval sold the livestock and machinery on the home farm. From 1923 to 1930 the house was empty; from 1930 to 1937 it was let to a Mr. Berridge, a retired tea planter, who carried out renovations and redecoration. In 1937 the house and remaining land were sold to the Land Commission and the State Forestry Department, the former's share being sub-divided among smallholders. The total acreage at the time was 18,000 and the price was £20,000. At the same time the contents of the house were separately sold. A contemporary newspaper report of the sale refers to the pictures, which consisted of family portraits and paintings of the Italian, Dutch and Flemish schools. Very few details are given of the library, save that it contained the statutes of Charles II and of the Irish Parliament, together with drawings and books on botany. Furniture, ceramics and statues were also sold.

During the second world war the house was occupied by the Irish army. In 1946, the war having ended, the Land Commission put the house only up for sale. The terms of the offer required the buyer to demolish the house, remove all materials and level the site. By way of encouragement the advertisement relating to the sale contained the information that the roof had a high quantity of lead. The announcement caused little apparent regret. The Irish Times commented:-"Hazelwood

House is going to be demolished and the people of Sligo, with exceptions, do not care".

Three days before the auction was due to take place the offer was withdrawn. A leading article in the Sligo Champion welcomed this decision and added:-

"The Land Commission specialises in the destruction of some of our most ornate buildings; whereas in England such houses are acquired by the National Trust, in Ireland the value of such a house is measured by the content of lead in the roof".

Later in the same year the Land Commission sold the house to St. Columba's Mental Hospital. After spending £4,000 on repairs the hospital for some years used the building as a home for mental patients.

Henry George L'Estrange died in 1929. When his widow, Mrs. Evelyn L'Estrange, died in 1952 the Sligo Champion commented that Sligo's last link with the Wynnes of Hazelwood had gone.

In 1969 an Italian company called Snia bought the house at Hazelwood with enough land to erect a factory. When built, the factory extended from the back elevation of the house to the shore of Lough Gill. This development obliterated the features mentioned in O'Rorke's description in 1889. At one time this company employed 500 persons at Hazelwood but in 1983, after production had ceased fourteen months previously, the factory finally closed. Four years later a South Korean company named Saehan Corporation, manufacturers of video tape, acquired the site. Reporting on this company's planning application, the Sligo Champion of the 5th August, 1988, stated:-

"The application outlines precisely what the video tape manufacturers have in mind for the Hazelwood site. It confirms that up to 500 jobs will be created initially, rising quickly to 800 once production is in full swing. Saehan will use most of the existing factory and will also be carrying out some additional building work. At a later stage they plan to restore the old Hazelwood House to its original condition for use as a residence and guest reception area".

In its issue of the 12th April, 1991 the Sligo Champion stated that the company had just completed a £13 million refurbishment of its 280,000 square feet factory and had installed £35 million worth of machinery and equipment. It anticipated that it could have 500 people employed by early 1992. The company is now the world's largest producer of video tapes.

HAZELWOOD IN 1992: THE NORTH FRONT

In the midst of this industrialisation something of the past survives. The woods around the factory retain their beauty. In 1985 the Hazelwood sculpture trail was inaugurated and a number of sculptures, carved of wood, stand among the trees. All are striking. One entitled *'Fergus Rules the Brazen Cars or Ghost Riders in the Sky'* is unforgettable. The sculptor has described it as a kind of dream-like procession flitting across one's line of vision to the shores of Lough Gill. This evokes the Ireland of myth and legend. Within the shorter time scale of this book , after nearly three hundred years of Anglo (or Welsh) - Irish Protestant ascendancy, Hazelwood has become the possession first of a European then of an Asiatic multi–national company. In those facts we may see much of the history of modern Ireland.

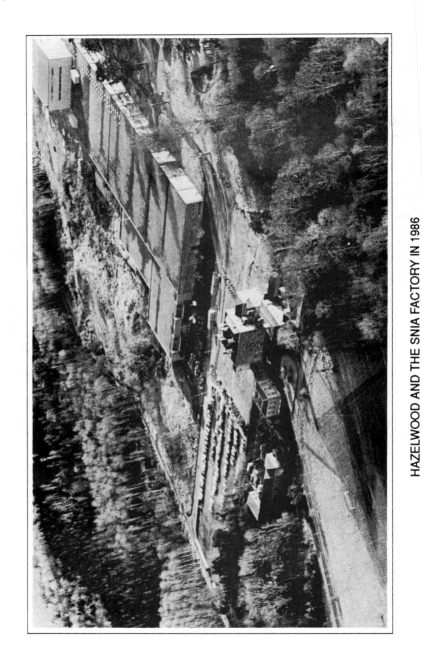

HAZELWOOD AND THE SNIA FACTORY IN 1986

PHOTO: COURESY OF THE SLIGO CHAMPION

APPENDIX

LIST OF TENANTS OF THE WYNNE ESTATE

The Primary Valuation of rateable property in Ireland, otherwise known as Griffith's Valuation, was carried out, as far as Counties Sligo and Leitrim are concerned, in the 1850's. The valuation was done in pursuance of the Irish Poor Law Act of 1838 which required it for the purpose of levying local rates in order to finance the relief of the poor.

The lists which follow are extracted from Griffiths' Valuation . The Map of County Leitrim shows the boundaries of the Civil Parishes with their names. In the map of County Sligo the Civil Parishes are numbered, the names of the Parishes being set out in the index to the map. In the lists the main headings refer to the parishes, followed by the names of Wynne's tenants in each townland. All the townlands appear on the newly published (1992) Ordnance Survey Maps (1:50,000), maps 16 and 25.

Civil Parishes
LEITRIM

Parishes in which
J.A. Wynne had property

LEITRIM TOWNLANDS

PARISH OF ROSSINVER

Cartrongibbagh
Daniel Meehan
Archibald Downey
Patrick Rogan
James Gilligan
Laurence Meehan
Edward McGurrin
James Gilligan
Cormick Gilligan
Michael McGurrin

Conray
Edward O'Neill
William Ferguson
John O'Rourke (Tim)
John O'Rourke (Hugh)
Denis O'Rourke
Hugh Sweeney
Patrick Kerrigan
Mary O'Rourke
James Clinton
Owen McGurrin
Anne Fox
Peter Sweeney
John Clinton
William Mc Caffrey
Mary Murray
John Murray

Coolodonnel
Michael Hart
Terence Kenny
John Fox
Bryan Dolan
John Robinson
Philip McKeon
Edward Gallagher

John McKeon
Edward McKeon
John Clarke

Corraleskin
Margaret Dolan
Patrick Maguire
Alexander Johnston
Bryan O'Rourke
Thomas Gallagher
James Gallagher
Terence Ferguson
Owen O'Rourke
John O'Rourke
Patrick O'Rourke
Hugh O'Rourke
John Ferguson
Margaret Ferguson
Francis O'Rourke
Denis Maguire

Derrynahimmirk
Margaret Boyde
Francis McGrath
Bartholomew Magrath
James Spear
Bartholomew Hart
Phelim Hart
Hugh Hart
Ellen Meehan
James Meehan
Bryan Gallagher
Myles McKeon
Percy Clarke
John Casson
William Ross

Drumgane
Michael O'Rourke

James O'Rourke
Rose Meehan
Michael Byrne

Gortnacrive
John Fox
William Ross
Thomas Connnolly
Hamilton Blair
Malachi Fox
Patrick Henery
Francis Trowers
John Fox

Gubmanus
John Sweeny
Andrew Ferguson
Philip Sweeney
Thomas Meehan
Owen Sweeney

Gubnageer
Hugh Ward
Patrick Skea
William Ferguson
Francis Gallagher
James Gallagher
Terence McGowan
Patrick Meehan
Felix Skea
William McGowan
Michael Cullen

Lattone
John Meehan
Patrick McGowan
Patrick O'Rourke
Terence Gallagher
Bridget Lannen
Celia Ferguson
James Bustard
Thomas Casson
Patrick Fox

James Owens
Patric Owens
Timothy Clancy
Patrick McLoughlin
Patrick McLoughlin
Patrick Maguire
Owen McMorrow
Bryan McGee
James Maguire
Susan Sweeney
John Gilfrader
Charles Meehan (little)
Charles Meehan (big)
Mary Maguire
Patrick Keoghan

Tullyderrin
Patrick Meehan
James Meehan
Lazarus Meehan
Michael Byrne
Francis McGowan
Patrick Flaherty

Shasmore
James Fox
Neill Fox

Kinkillew
Daniel Mc Keon
James McKeon
Philip McKeon
Lawrence Meehan
Darby Meehan
Ellen McGowan
Patrick Evans

Lisdarush
Thomas Irwin
Thoams Connolly
Hamilton Blair

Jane Hurst
Anne Hurst
James Gallagher
Mary Gallagher
Francis Fox
Terence Ferguson
John Fox
Patrick Fox
Owen Dolan
Bryan Dolan
John Dolan
Mary Fox
Dominick Hart
James Fox

Raheelin

Samuel McParlan
Henry Ferguson
Owen McParlan
Eliza Mc Parlan
John Cox
James Meehan
Lazarus Connolly
Paul Mulhern
Margaret McSharry
George Ferguson
James McGowan
John McGowan
Michael Rooney
Charles McLoughlin
Kate Sweeney
Francis Sweeney

Gortnaderry

Owen Magourty
Thomas Maguire
Henry Ferguson
Terence Maguire
Patrick Dolan
Bryan Ferguson
John Ferguson

Patrick Ferguson
Grace Ward
Daniel Ward
Myles Gordon
Hugh Meehan
Bernard Ferguson
Patrick O'Rourke
Bridget Mitchel
Thomas Meehan
Felix Meehan
John Meehan

Tullyskehenry

Edward Gilgunn
James Gallagher
Thomas Gallagher
Paul Clancy
Denis Maguire
Thomas Maguire
Terence Hart
Peter Hart
Patrick Gilroy
Patrick McNulty
Bridget McNulty
John McNulty
John Hurst
Patrick Monahan
Peter Gordon
Sarah Monahan
Patrick Gilligan
Hugh O'Rourke
Michael Tucker
Patrick Tucker
John Robinson
John Irwin
Barbara Saunderson
William Saunderson
John Whittaker

Druminargid

Bryan O'Rourke
Hugh O'Rourke
Patrick Keenan
Bryan O'Rourke jnr
David Brockes
James Elliot
Owen Shea

PARISH OF CLOONLOUGHER

Cloonlougher

John Conlon
Michael Mourne
William Conboy
Henry Sibberry
Ellen Gallagher
Loughlin Gallagher

Gortgarrigan

James Kearney
Henry Nicholson
James Clifford
Hugh McGovern
James McLoughlin
William McLoughlin
Mary Flinn
Michael Hart
Matthew Walsh

Cloonaquin

James McHugh
Michael McDermott
Partick McDermott
Thomas McDermott
Bridget Lynch
Michael McHugh
John Fox
Owen McDermott
Michael McDermott
John Mc Cordock

Hugh Clancy
John Mc Glone
George Crawford
Henry Stewart
John Middleton
Honor Mullaniffe
Catherine Mullaniffe
Bernard McGeniskin (Clooniquin)
John Denison
Michael Bradley
James Bradley
Patrick McMurray
John McMurray
James Brannan

Poll Boy

Martin Eames
Richard Crown
John Eames
Owen Flynn
Philip MaGuire
James Henry
James McMurray
Patrick McMurray

Srabrick

John Saunderson
James Armstrong
William Armstrong
John McGlone
Robert Wilson

PARISH OF DRUMLEASE

Kinnara Glebe

Francis Harte
James Harte
James Smith

Boihy

John Denison

John Bradley
James Bradley
Henry Duncan
Adam Johnson
Anne Dawson

PARISH OF KILLANUMMERY

Darby Brennan
John Cosgrave
Dorothy Cournan
Peter Carty
James Banks
Lancelot Johnston
Philip Dolan
John O'Boyle (Killanummery)
Patrick Higgins
Mary Hart
Henry Banks
Mary Rutledge

PARISH OF KILLASNET

Ballyglass

Patrick Gaffney
Alick Mc Daniel
Thomas Lynott
Bridget Keegan
Francis McCann
Hugh Smith
John McGlone
Thomas Siberry
William Frazer
James Lindsay
Robert Davis

Barrickpark

Christopher Armstrong
James Lindsay
Colles James

Gortinar

William Smith

Patrick Lynch
William Ritchie
Terence Feely
Patrick Feely
Bridget Feely
John Mulhern
Robert McAnassar
James Clarke
Hamilton Sharpe
William Dixon
John Pye
William Sharpe
Robert Fletcher
John McAnassar
Malcolm Sharpe
James Sharpe
Mary Hunt

Largandoon

Robert Boyde
Denis Mitchel
Thomas Siberry
George Allingham

Part of
Lurganboy Village & Barrickpark

Capt. H.H.Slade
James Lindsay
William Frazer
Mary Anne McKenny
Colles James
Margaret McLoughlin
John James
William Duffy
James Mc Daniel
George Porteus
Edward McLoughlin
Susanna Lyte
Robert Davis
Irwin Siberry

Corglass

George Allingham
Patrick Brennan
Bartley Rooneen
Thomas Mc Sharry

Gortnagrogerny

William Henry
Duncan Denison
Thomas Denison

Knocknaclasagh

Henry Fletcher
Christine Rooney
William Allingham
Duncan Brett
John Ferguson
Thomas Allingham

Meenaphuill

Henry Fletcher
Anne Fletcher
Edward Earles
John McBryan
John Monaghan

Mountainthird

Christopher Armstrong
Edward Siberry
James Lindsay
James Sharkey
Capt..H.Slade

Sracreeghan

Duncan Brett
John Ferguson
Thomas Allingham
John Allingham
George Allingham
William Middleton
Thomas Middleton
James Middleton

Catherine Middleton

Treanakillew

John Hart
Patrick McEnroy
Malachy Carty
John Scanlon
Denis Mitchell
John Fallon

Milltown

James Davis
Robert Armstrong
John Wallace
William Peacock

Nure

David Clarke
Walker Sharpe
Benjamin Armstrong
Duncan Campbell
Thomas Dermott
Patrick Gaffney
James Gaffney
Denis Rooneen

Poundhill

John James
James Lindsay
Anthony Crown
Robert Davis

Shanvaus

John McGloin
Alexander Roycroft
Dominick Gonelly
William Ross
Robert Davis
John Rogers

Twigspark

Christopher Armstrong

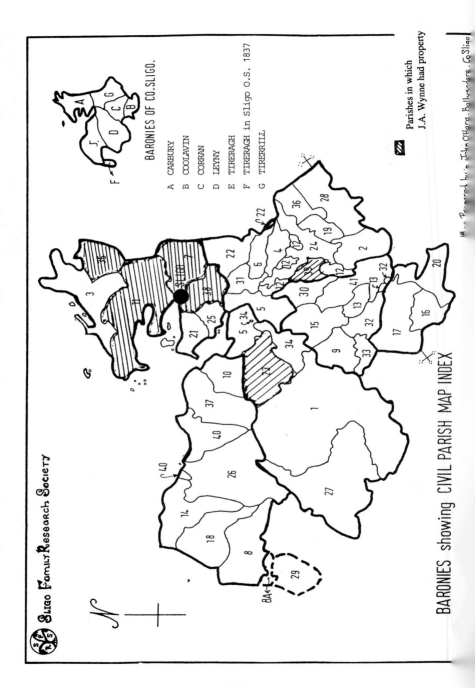

Sligo Family Research Society

BARONIES OF CO. SLIGO.

A CARBURY
B COOLAVIN
C CORRAN
D LEYNY
E TIRERAGH
F TIRERAGH in Sligo O.S. 1837
G TIRERRILL

▨ Parishes in which
J.A. Wynne had property

Map Prepared by : John O'Hara, Ballysadare, Co Sligo.

BARONIES showing CIVIL PARISH MAP INDEX

102

CIVIL PARISH INDEX TO CO. SLIGO.

PARISH		BARONY
1	ACHONRY	LEYNY
2	AGHANAGH	TIRERRILL
3	AHAMLISH	CARBURY
4	BALLYNAKILL	TIRERRILL
5	BALLYSADARE	LEYNY & TIRERRILL
6	BALLYSUMAGHAN	TIRERRILL
7	CALRY	CARBURY
8,8A	CASTLECONOR	TIRERAGH
9	CLOONOGHIL	CORRAN
10	DROMARD	TIRERAGH
11	DRUMCLIFF	CARBURY
12	DRUMCOLUMB	TIRERRILL
13	DRUMRAT	CORRAN
14	EASKY	TIRERAGH
15	EMLAGHFAD	CORRAN

PARISH		BARONY
16	KILCOLMAN	COOLAVIN
17	KILFREE (Part of)	COOLAVIN
18	KILGLASS	TIRERAGH
19	KILLADOON	TIRERRILL
20	KILLARAGHT	COOLAVIN
21	KILLASPUGBRONE	CARBURY
22	KILLERRY	TIRERRILL
23	KILLORAN	LEYNY
24	KILMACALLAN	TIRERRILL
25	KILMACOWEN	CARBURY
26	KILMACSHALGAN	TIRERAGH
27	KILMACTEIGE	LEYNY
28	KILMACTRANNY	TIRERRILL
29	KILMOREMOY (O.S. 1837) (Part of)	TIRERAGH
30	KILMORGAN	CORRAN

CIVIL PARISH INDEX TO CO. SLIGO.

PARISH		BARONY
31	KILROSS	TIRERRILL
32	KILSHALVY	CORRAN
33	KILTURRA	CORRAN & COSTELLO
34	KILVARNET	LEYNY
35	ROSSINVER (Part of)	CARBURY
36	SHANCOUGH	TIRERRILL
37	SKREEN	TIRERAGH
38	St. JOHNS	CARBURY
39	TAWNAGH	TIRERRILL
40	TEMPLEBOY	TIRERAGH
41	TOOMOUR	CORRAN

103

SLIGO TOWNLANDS

PARISH OF DRUMCLIFF

Ballynagaliagh

John Crystlo
John Fawley
Robert Munds
William Shaw
John Frizell
Mary O'Connor
Michael O'Connor
Smyth Shaw jnr
William Stewart
James Shaw jnr
Edward Munds
James Shaw snr
Mark Devin
Thomas Nicholson
Smyth Shaw snr
William Simpson
George Shaw
Robert Shaw
Bridget Brierly
Thomas Yeates

Ballincar

John Wynne
Edward Simpson
Moses Monds
Robert McBride
William Barber
Thomas Yeates
Capt.Michael Jones
William Young
Robert Clarke
Michael Tully
Daniel Clarke
Frances Bruen

Robert Hunter snr
David Lindsay
William Little
Robert Hunter jnr

Cloonderry

William Carr sen
Patrick Carr
George Carr jnr
William Carr
Hannah Carr
James Carr
George Carr
George Carr sen
James Carr sen

Clooneen

William Munds
John Frizell
John Brett
Michael Regan jnr
James Frizell
Denis Boyle
Thomas Frizell
John West
Michael Regan snr
John Tynan
James Costello
James Carr
George Carr
Hannah Carr

Cloonmull

Michael Regan jnr
Smyth Shaw
Edmund Munds

PARISH OF DRUMCLIFF

Cregg
James Feeny
Martin Meeny
Thomas Yeates
George Banks
James Algo
Robert Pye
Patrick Carroll
Robert Mc Bride
William Barber
Edward Bruen
Robert Clarke
Thomas Ward
John Curran
William Adams
Capt.Alex Lumsden
Robert Hunter
Robert Lynd M.D.
Robert Wilson
Rev.Patrick O'Gara
Patrick Keighron

Drumkilsillagh
Phillip Parke
Robert Shaw
John Parke
Duncan Denison
Isabelle Shannon

Lisnalurg
Francis Oliphant
John Gowan
Patrick Brennan
Robert Hunter
Robert Whiteside
George Jas. Robinson

Kiltycooly
James Carr

Robert Armstrong
Robert Hunter
Patrick Hart
Michael Scanlan
John Armatrong
James Kerr

Kilsellagh
David Frizell
John Cullen
John Coleman
David Cullen
Robert Long
Elenor Hall
Alisha O'Connor
Thomas Frizell
James Williams
Elizabeth Williams
Joseph Browne
Robert Shaw
Margaret Buckard
Duncan Denison

Mullaghnaneane
John Stewart
Thomas Stewart
Thomas Carty
Robert Hendry
Mathew Lyth
Patrick Lindsay
William Lindsay
James Lindsay
Robert Gregg
Samuel Gregg
Martin Regan
Roger Gilmore
Anne Payne
Christopher Gilmore
Joseph Barber
Charles Hendry
James Hendry

Samuel Gregg
Mary Kilmartin
Thomas Lindsay
John Payne
William McFadden
Rebecca Lindsay
James Regan

Tully
John Carr
Dorah Mackey
Young Shaw
Olivia Simpson
Follis Clarke
Charles Simpson
James Lynch
William Jameson
Patrick Oates
Elenor Henderson

Drumm East
George Carr
Patrick Hart
Michael Carroll
Philip Shaw
John Parke

Drum West
Hannah Carr
Robert Cunningham
George Cunningham
George Carr
Edward Cunningham
John Cahill
William Carr

Ballinvoher
Francis M Olpherts

William Young
Robert Whiteside
William Lytle
Robert Hunter Jnr
James Clarke
Robert Hunter Snr
John Seberry

Ballyweelin
John Carr
Philip Wilson
John Wynne
William Carr
Robert Wilson
Capt. Alex Lumsden
Thomas Crawley

Sligo Bay
Adjacent to Ballyweelin
John Wynne

PARISH OF KILLORAN

Moylough
David Lilly
James McNulty snr
James McNulty jnr
Henry Burrows

PARISH OF KILLERRY
Correagh
Martin McGarry
Patrick Cregg
John Wynne
Mathew Savage

Islands in Lough Gill
Henry Griffith (Innishfree)
John Wynne

3lishwood

John Wynne
Martin McGarry
Patrick Cregg
James Cregg

PARISH OF TAWNAGH

Behy

William Slator

Thomas Slator
John Slator
Thomas Barber
Edward Rowlett
William Rowlett
James Rowlett
Margaret O'Connor

PARISH OF CALRY

Carncash

Andrew McCullagh
George Warren Shaw
Michael Brennan
Mathew Rowlet
James Kerr
James Gillen
Catherine Gillen
Francis Commons

Shannon Eighter

Francis M. Olpherts
John Duncan
William Little
Robert Hunter

Barroe

John Hart
William Rowlett
Follis Clarke

Patrick Boyde
Michael Creen
Martin Foley
Mary Healy
Bryan Mitchell
Catherine Foley
Thomas Murray
John Wynne

Carrowlustia

Richard Mc Cullagh
William Shaw
Robert Henry
John Fletcher
Owen Clarke
Patrick Hopper
John McSharry
Patrick McSharry
Owen Clarke

Doonally

Roger Parke

Colgagh

William Fox

Clougher Beg

Follis Clarke
Jane Parke

Fermoyle

Warren Henry
James McGoldrick
Owen McGoldrick
Andrew Henry
Patrick Connolly
Charles Anderson
William Fox
James Frazer
Peter Feeney

Rose Feeney
James Pye
Patrick Gilligan
George Armstrong
Michael McAnasser
John McAnasser
George Armstrong
John Sheridan
Bridget Sheridan
Martin Feeney
Patrick Giligan
Charles Short
Patrick Sheridan
John Scanlon
Denis O'Connor
Michael Sheridan
John Hart

Ballure

Hugh Gillgan
Philip Gillgan
John Flynn
Patrick Devanny
James McLoughlin
Michael Wynne
Thomas McLoughlin
Patrick McLoughlin
William McLoughlin
James Commons
Patrick Blake
Michael Scanlan
Mary Black
John Hopper

Ballyglass

Rev.William Gillmore

Ballynamona

Martin Feeny, sen
Patrick Gillgan

Martin Feeny Jnr
James Feeny
John Feeny (Big)
John McGuinn
Patrick Hart
Patrick Boey
John Boey
Patrick Cunningham
William McGoldrick
James Hopper

Bellanurly

Anne Holmes
John Browne
Patrick Meehan snr
Patrick Meehan jnr
Michael Rogan
Farrell Moore
Thomas Gilligan

Clougher More

James Hopper
James Heraghty
John Wynne
Thomas Coristine
Honoria Hopper
James Patterson

Clogherrevagh

Mary Brennan
James Hopper
Thomas Heraghty
Mary Brennan

Cornwillick

Follis Clarke
Michael Hargadon
William Cunningham
Martin Feeny
Michael Burns

Patrick Burns
John Wynne

Faughts

George Henry
Roger Parke
Thomas Henry
John Patterson
Phillip Parke
William Clarke
John Wynne
Patrick Campbell
Thomas Staunton
Luke Derrig
Hugh Devanny
Bridget Kennedy
Luke Carroll
James Dunne
Catherine McGoldrick

Kiltycahill

Patrick Barry
Mary Commins
William Clancy
Thomas Fox
William Rowlett
William Gethin
Patrick Kilbride
Owen Commons
Thomas Gallagher
John Hart
Peter Gillin
James Carroll

PARISH OF CALRY

Magheraghan Rush or Deerpark

John Wynne
James Frazer

Tully

William McGoldrick
Patrick Boey
Michael Hargedon
Thomas McGowan
James McGowan
Patrick Feeny snr
Rose Feeny
Patrick Boey
Patrick Hargadon jnr
Patrick Hargadon snr
John Wynne

Ballytivnan

Follis Clarke

Hazelwood Demesne

John Wynne

Rathbraghan

Patrick Hart
Dr. James Ferguson
William Rowlet
Follis Clarke
John Derrig
Robert Lindsay

UNION OF SLIGO

St.John's

Aghamore Near

Thaddeus Oates
Luke Oates
William McManus
Patrick Carty
Patrick Dunbar
Francis McFadden
Michael Dunbar
John Gallagher
Michael Melly

Terence Rourke
Owen McLoughlin
Patrick McLoughlin

St John's
Lahanagh
Charles Harrison
Luke Cesnan
Martin Mulvy
Martin Kilroy
Malachi Gilligan
Bryan Cesnan
Owen Gallagher
Patrick Oates
Patrick Mulvey

NORTH WARD

Calry Ballytivnan
Dr Edward Powell
John West jnr
Farrell Conlan
George Beatty Wk.House
John Wynne Fair grn.
         Lunatic Asy
         Fairs & Marts
Robert Lindsay
Follis Clarke
James Hart
John Derrig
John Armstrong
Patrick Keighron
Harpur Campbell
Vernon Davis
Jackson Thorence
John Parkes

Calry Bellanode
Mary Little
James Hamilton

John Meehan
Margaret Tarpy
Margaret Buckard
John Wynne
Michael O'Connor
Charles Anderson
WilliamClarke
James Rowlet
Thomas Hennessy
Isaac Charlton

Rathquarter
John Kearns
Rev.William Hoops
William Clarke
Owen Wynne
Thomas Henry (Hospitals)
John Wynne (Work House)
Harpur Campbell
Rathquarter The Mall
Isaac Charlton
Alexander Phillips
John Derrig
Thomas Mostyn
William Gethin
Margaret Kerr
Andrew Weir

EAST WARD ST JOHN'S

Abbeyquarter South
Robert Mc Bride

Abbeyquarter West
Robert McBride

WEST WARD ST JOHN'S

Village of Magheraboy
John Moffatt
Charles Cornton
James Wallace

Hugh Rooney
Dr Jas. Ferguson
Stephen Hughes

Church Lane
Presbyterian Church
Rev Edward Day

The Lungy
James Burrows
Rev Edward Day

West Ward
James Wallace
Michael Foley
James Rooney
William A Woods

Knocknaganny
William A Woods

Pound St
John Lavin
Michael Millmore
Patrick Hughes
Henry Mulligan
John O'Donnell
Bernard O'Flynn
Thady McNamara
James OFlynn
James Shaw
Bridget McCawley

Market St. West Side
John Henry

High St. West Side
Patrick Kerr
Thomas Little

Thomas H Williams
Edward Chism
R.C. Friary
Thady Kilgallon
John Lavin
MichaelMillmore
Patrick Hughes
Henry Mulligan
John O'Donnell
Bernard Flynn
Thady McNamara
James O Flynn
James Shaw
Bridget McCauley

North Ward
School House

Stephen St.
Wesleyan Church & yard
Independent Church & School
Thady McNamara
James O'Flynn
James Shaw
Bridget McCauley

BALLISODARE

Kinnagrelly
John Burke
Patrick Burke sen
Patrick Goulding
Terence Burke
Michael Burke
Patrick Burke jnr
Patrick Kevany
John McKeon

List of Labourers
1833 May 4th

1. Pat Berrig
2. Pat McGuin
3. James Duffy
4. Thos Foy
5. Luke Berrig
6. Pat Scanton
7/8. Mich Campbell
8. Thos Carroll
9. James Foley
10. Lanl Dunn
11. Pat Foy
12. Wm Boyd
13. Mich Freel
14. Thos Hargaden
15. Thos Commons
16. Hugh McIna
17. Joe Denby McCormick
18. Shady McCormick
19. Samuel Boyd
20. Pat Campbell
21. Martin Foley
22. James Commons
23. John Gallagher
24. Prt Gallagher
25. Phylimy Hargaden
26. John Murtough
27. Pat Healy
28. Pat Carroll
29. James Kerr
30. James Scott
31. John Gallacher
32. James Kast
33. Pat Blake
34. John Flynn
35. Wm Wood
36. Mich Clarke
37. Owen Clarke
38. Owen Commons
39. Mich Commons
40. Frank Hopper
41. John Collery
42. Andrew Berrig
43. Pat Campbell senr
44. Pat Black
45. Mich Hopper
46. James Hopper
47. James Dunn
48. Mich Foley
49. James Mulligan
50. James Curry
51. John Curry
52. Edwd Healy
53. Bryan Mitchell
54. Frank Carroll
55. Thos Carroll
56. Peter Foy
57. Peter Scanlon
58. Thos Murtough
59. Thos Dunn
60. Pat Curry
61. Pat Duffy
62. Pat Boyd
63. Mich May
64. Wm Scott
65. John Dunn
66. Thos Curry
67. James McGloughlin
68. Lacky Scanlon
69. Pat Carroll
70. Pat Devans
71. Robt Scott